Winter Warmers

Clare Bevan

*For Dear Cynthia,
With Love.
Have Fun.
Clare Bevan*

Published by New Generation Publishing in 2022

Copyright © Clare Bevan 2022

First Edition

The author asserts the moral right under the Copyright, Designs and Patents Act 1988 to be identified as the author of this work.

All Rights reserved. No part of this publication may be reproduced, stored in a retrieval system or transmitted, in any form or by any means without the prior consent of the author, nor be otherwise circulated in any form of binding or cover other than that which it is published and without a similar condition being imposed on the subsequent purchaser.

ISBN   978-1-80369-464-1

www.newgeneration-publishing.com

New Generation Publishing

INTRODUCTION.
****

From Clare Bevan.

Welcome to my 'Winter Warmers' Christmas Poems. (Part One!)

So - pull on a Jolly Jumper; look out for a Single Star; don't forget to buy your Christmas Cards, then enjoy a few Carol Singers too.

Some of the 'First Christmas' poems have a slightly adult feel – but only Herod is complaining! And of course, Father Christmas is already packing his sleigh, so along the way, you'll find plenty of festive fun.

****

They tell me my singing is painful,
I sound like a twanging of wire -
Or finger-nails scratching down windows...
And now I've been sacked from the Choir.

They told me I shouldn't try Carols,
They told me that crime wouldn't pay...
But look! I've collected a fortune
In bribes - just to keep me away.

****

This book is dedicated to all my wonderful
Readers and Musicians.
You are Heroes all!

****

A BIG CHRISTMAS 'THANK YOU' PAGE.
****

First:
An enormous thank you to all my wonderful Readers.

The lovely Bracknell Drama Club Crew who have always read my poems so splendidly - plus special thanks to Ann and Roger, who turned my little Christmas collections into jolly-holly booklets.

All our brilliant Musicians, especially: Bea, John, Tim and Kim.

All the brave children who sang along and enjoyed the fun !

And of course, dear old Ted who knew Father Christmas so well.

****

Second:
All the friends and fans who have come along to our 'Poems and Pies' shows.

Some of you have been to EVERY show since 1985!

And now our new audiences and readers in friendly Crowthorne.

You have helped us raise a great deal of money for our local families, who are coping with Muscular Dystrophy - thank you SO much.

****

Third:
Our 'Poems and Pies' friends from all over the country:
Axmouth; Canterbury; Ian Tracey and Readers from Liverpool Cathedral; Stockport; The Wirral; Orkney; London; Croydon; Stowupland, Henley and more.

****

Fourth
Famous Friends - especially Sir Richard Baker, who used my poems at the Barbican and on B.B.C. Radio Four - and gave me some merry ideas.

Dear Sir Ken Dodd and Lady Anne Dodd, who inspired so many of my favourite poems. Ken's festive voice is on our Answer Phone - so he can still give me a nudge when it's time to start a new set of cheery poems.

****

And finally, Martin and Ben - who have not only performed their poems brilliantly, but have also put out the chairs for the audience...and cleared up afterwards!

(More importantly, Martin is now our contact with good old Santa Claus!)

>THANK YOU ALL.

****

(And if this book sells well, some of my profits will go to Muscular Dystrophy U.K.)

Winter Warmers Contents

ONE STAR 1

STARS OF WONDER 3
LISTEN. 4
THE DONKEY'S SONG. 5
THE DONKEY'S CHRISTMAS TALE. 6
THE CARPENTER'S SONG. 8
THE LAMB'S STORY. 10
THE SHEPHERD BOY'S STORY. 11
THE SHEPHERD'S DOG. 12
THE ANGEL. 15
THE PAGE-BOY'S POEM. 16
THE THREE WISE WIVES. 18
GIFTS FOR THE BABY. 20
BABOUSHKA'S LAMENT. 22
HEROD'S STORY. 24
A NOVEL NATIVITY. 26
THE CHRISTMAS WREATH. 28
THE CHRISTMAS BABY. 29
ONE STAR. 31

WINTER WARMERS 32

WINTER WARMERS................................33
THE JOLLY JUMPER POEM........................34
THE CHRISTMAS KNITTER........................36
BIRD TABLE BLUES. 38
GARDENING TIPS. 40
FLIGHT OF FANCY. 42
SNOW TIME! 43
SNOW PROBLEM......................................45
AFTER THE SNOW. 46
THE LONELIEST SNOWMAN........................47
SNOW JOKE...48
THE SNOWY SUFFRAGETTES......................50
SONG OF A CAT WHO HAS JUST
DISCOVERED SNOW. 51
A SHIVER OF WINGS................................52
WHEREVER DID ALL THE WHITE..............53
CHRISTMASES GO? 53
A THANK YOU NOTE. 54
THE CHRISTMAS HEROES. 56
DECEMBER DILEMMA. 58
THE VISITATION......................................60
HERE IS THE NEWS. 61
THE CHRISTMAS CONJUROR......................63

AN ADVENTUROUS ADVENT 65

THE ADVENT CALENDAR............................ 66
AN ADVENTUROUS ADVENT. 67
THE CHILDREN'S ADVENT CALENDAR.. 69
CHRISTMAS CARD QUESTIONNAIRE. 70
MERRY MAIL? 72
A FESTIVE CONFUSION. 73
THE CHRISTMAS NEWS BLUES. 75
SANTA'S CHRISTMAS NEWS BLUES. 77
ALL LIT UP. 79
CANDLE COMPLAINT. 81
CHRISTMAS LIGHTS....................................... 83
THE CHRISTMAS FAIRY-LIGHTS. 84
(Three Quick Christmas Carols.) 84
THE CAROL SINGER'S STORY. 87
HARK THE HORRID. 87
ONE MORE TIME FOR ME. 88
DECEMBER SONG.. 90
BAH HUMBUG! 92
MUSIC HATH CHARMS. 94
SWEET SINGING IN THE CHOIR. 95
.MERRY MUSAK. 97
AWAY FROM IT ALL. 98

DEAR OLD DECORATIONS..........................99

CHRISTMAS TREE CAT. 100
THE CHRISTMAS TREE FAIRY.................101
THE FAIRY IN THE LOFT......................103
I'M DREAMING OF A GREEN CHRISTMAS. 105
SNOWFLAKES. 107
THE BAY TREE. 108
POT PLANT PROBLEM. 110
OUR BEAUTIFUL POT PLANT. 111
OUR CRAZY CHRISTMAS. 112
THE BIRD IN THE TREE. 114
WE WISH YOU A THRIFTY CHRISTMAS.116
THE WRAPPING PAPER WRAP.................118
THE PERFECT PRESENT WRAPPER. 120
THE CHRISTMAS BAZAAR. 121
THE CHOICE...123
THE CHRISTMAS RAFFLE............................124
THE THIEF IN THE SHOP. 125
BREADLINE BLUES. 126
A MERRY RECESSION. 128
THE HAMPER. 130
HAPPINESS HAMPERS DOT COM............132

CHRISTMAS COMPANY 134

> REINDEER RAP. 135
> 'TIS THE SEASON FOR A SELFIE. 136
> RUDOLPH'S BACK. 138
> WHAT SHALL WE DO WITH THE RED-
> NOSED REINDEER.. 140
> THE CHRISTMAS CONTEST. 142
> THE POLAR BEAR POEM. 144
> DRONING ON. 145
> THE ELF AND SAFETY RAP. 146
> E. L. F. 147
> THE IGLOO BLUES... 148
> SANTA'S SOLILOQUY.................................... 149
> A CLOSE SHAVE... 151
> 'TIS THE SEASON TO BE HAIRY. 153
> THE SANTA SCHOOL RAP......................... 155
> SANTA'S SPOOKY CHRISTMAS................ 157
> JUST A NOTE AT TWILIGHT. 159
> IF YOU GO DOWN TO THE MALL
> TODAY... 160
> MOTHER CHRISTMAS................................. 162
> A MERRY MUDDLE. 163

TALES BY TORCH-LIGHT..............................165

A WINTER'S TALE. 166
THE GHOST HORSES. 167
CHRISTMAS AT HOME. 168
THE STRANGER'S STORY..........................170
FOOTPRINTS IN THE SNOW. 172
THE CRY. 174
THE PHANTOM RIDER................................175
THE ROLLRIGHT STONES..........................177
THE CHIME CHILD. 179
THE LISTENERS OF CLASS THIRTEEN. 180
THE SINGERS OF ORCHARD CLOSE........181
THE POEM IN YOUR HAND. 183
'TIS THE SEASON TO BE SCARY..............185
THE HORRIBLE HAUNTING OF FIFI MOULD...187
THE FRIDGE ON THE STAIR. 188
CHRISTMAS PAST..190
THE GHOST OF CHRISTMAS PAST. 191

ONE STAR

STARS OF WONDER
****

(Adult Version)

When the Shepherds ran
From a dazzle of light.
When voices followed their downward flight,
A friendly star
Made their pathway bright.

When the Wise Men wandered
Too long, too far,
When the wind grew harsh as a battle-scar,
They turned their gaze
To a patient star.

When the Family fled
From a deadly crown,
When terrors were stalking each trail, each town -
A comforting star
Shone softly down.

When Mariners dreaded
The snarling storm,
When waves rose up in a demon's form,
A faithful star
Kept their courage warm.

And when you're lost,
When your dreams fall through;
When nothing in life seems good. Or true.
Look up. Find the Star
That shines
For you.

****

LISTEN.
****

(Adult Version)

Listen.
Far away, the snort of a camel;
The swish of boots in the endless sand;
The whisper of silk and the clatter
Of ceremonial swords,
Far away.

Listen.
Not so far, the slam of a castle door;
A cry of rage on the midnight air;
A jangle of spurs and the cold thrust
Of a soldier's command,
Not so far.

Listen.
Closer now, the homely bleat of a ewe
Among the grasses;
The answering call of her lamb, fresh born;
The rattle of stones on a hillside path,
Closer now.

Listen.
Nearer still, the murmer of women in the dark;
The kindly creak of a stable door;
The steady breathing of the sleepy beasts,
Nearer still.

Listen.
Can you hear the father's sigh?
The singing of the stars;
The soundless flurry of wings;
The soft whimper of a child amongst the straw,
So close
You are almost there.
****

THE DONKEY'S SONG.
****

The donkey plodded past Bethlehem hill,
The road was hard
and the way was long;
The stars in the Heaven were bright and still,
His back grew sore,
but his heart was strong.

The oxen groaned in the stable gloom,
The road was hard
and the way was long;
For a working beast there is always room,
And here can a faithful
soul belong.

In the gathering dark the child was born -
The road was hard
and the way was long.
But the breath of a donkey was soft and warm,
And a kindly beast
heard a joyful throng.

Then a moonbeam circled his patient crown,
The road was hard
and the way was long;
While all the stars in the sky looked down
And his weary voice
was filled with song.

****

THE DONKEY'S CHRISTMAS TALE.
****

One winter, when journeys were harder than now,
A man asked his neighbour to help him. Somehow.
"My friend," said the farmer. "I'll lend you my donkey -
He's willing and keen,
But a tiny bit wonky!"

"So he's not the best choice for a travelling man,
But he'll carry your lady as well as he can."
The woman was weary and ready to drop,
So she climbed on the beast
And his hoofs went clip-clop.

But since all his legs were assorted in size
Poor Mary felt seasick. She covered her eyes
And she tried not to groan as she wobbled about,
Though pathways were rocky,
Directions in doubt.

At last, they arrived at an Inn - shut and barred.
The donkey went: "Hee-Haw!" He clopped round the yard.
Till the Inn-Keeper shouted: "If someone is able -
To silence that donkey
I'll lend you my stable."

Well, the shelter was cosy and peace seemed to reign -
Until the daft donkey went: "Hee-Haw!" again.
He was trying to nibble the hay in the manger,
So the oxen (quite rightly)
Were nudging the stranger.

But hush! They heard cries like an anthem of joy,
And there, in the straw, lay a new baby boy!
And even the donkey grew quiet just then -
While someone above him
Sang softly: 'Amen.'

The Inn-Keeper's wife came with blankets and bread;
There were shepherds. And camels. And Kings (it is said).
But the donkey who tried to be faithful and strong,
Remembered that journey
So hard and so long...

And the brush of a feather.
An Angel's sweet song.

****

THE CARPENTER'S SONG.
****

Joseph stood in the moonlight,
His shame as sharp as an awl;
And he grieved for the newborn mother
Who nursed her child in a stall.

"Where are the fruits of the forest
I promised to spread at your feet?
Where is the chair carved from cedar,
The love-spoon of sandal-wood sweet?
Where is the ebony bracelet
Dark as a Bethlehem sky?
Where is the plaything of beechwood
To comfort the little one's cry?"

"Where are the toys made from balsa
Softened and and rounded with sand?
Where is the cherrywood cradle
To rock with a gentling hand?
All I have brought you is hardship,
Curling like dross on the floor;
The splintered friendship of strangers,
The curse of a thrice barred door."

Mary sat in the moonlight,
Her smile was as quick as a blade -
And her touch was as soothing as beeswax,
Knowing his soul was afraid.

"Your arms are warm as the cedar,
And sweet is the trust we share;
The ebony gleam of your courage
Is the keepsake I would wear;
The healing softness of patience
To banish the little one's tears;

And love far stronger than cherry
Shall carry us safe through the years."

"All these treasures you brought me,
Scenting the path where we trod -
Why else did you think you were chosen,
To foster the firstborn of God."

****

THE LAMB'S STORY.
****

I was the weak rejected one -
Left for the crows
To have their fun.

The shepherd's wife, she took me in
Kept me warm
With her own, soft skin.
Now I am tame as a little child,
Bleating at boys
On the hilltop wild.

Taking my food from anyone's hand,
Free as a dog
In the midnight land.
But men with wings are a mystery -
Their song so strange
It startles me.

I follow the crowd to a secret place,
I watch the mother's
Weary face.
Around her feet I softly twine,
To share my warmth
Where cold stars shine.

Her baby's cry is weak and thin -
May gentle strangers
Take him in.
And when the human crows arrive,
May kindness keep
Her lamb alive.

****

THE SHEPHERD BOY'S STORY.

They left me here on the hillside,
Old Sam and the rest of the men.
I watched out for wolves in the moonlight,
I guarded the ewes in their pen.

I sat there alone on the hillside
And fashioned a pipe from a reed -
The village grew silent and sleepy,
The flocks were too drowsy to feed.
The stars had gone down from the hillside
But shadows were stalking my soul -
The rocks became devils and demons,
The vale was a fathomless hole.

I shivered with fear on the hillside,
And reached for the pipe I had made.
I would not abandon my duty,
For all I was small and afraid.
I fought with my fear on the hillside,
And lifted the pipe in my hands,
The tune that I played was a magic
From faraway, beautiful lands.

When Sam called my name on the hillside
And ordered me home with the rest,
I followed the path to the stable
Still clutching my pipe to my chest...
And there, in a cave by the hillside
A mother and baby lay curled,
Who smiled as I knelt in the starlight...
As I gave them
My wonderful world.

THE SHEPHERD'S DOG.
****

I'm well trained, me.
Come when I'm called,
Sit, stay, beg for scraps,
Roll over dead -
All that showy stuff.
Plus, of course, my qualifications.
You name it,
I'll round it up.
No matter how stupid the sheep,
How springy the lamb,
How belligerent the ram -
Into the field they go,
No trouble.
And as for strangers -
It's: "Clear off or I'll open your throat for you,
And no questions asked."

It's a talent I suppose,
I always win -
Until last week...

It was the long, yawning hours before dawn.
I was curled against a rock as usual -
One ear awake.
The flock was drowsy,
Just the occasional belch.
Even the fire burned lazily...
The all Hell broke loose.

The sky was a whirlpool of lights, noises, flailing wings.
The smell of fear stung my nostrils
And I would have tasted foreign flesh
If it hadn't been for the voices.

Down I went
On my obedient haunches -
A statue disguised in quivering fur,
While my Master whimpered like a whipped puppy.

When it was dark again,
I trailed after the boys,
My dishonoured tail dragging in the mud.
I should have swept those shining ones into the gully,
Ripped their starry robes
Until the air was full of feathers.

But I slunk inside the stable,
Expecting a cuff from my Master's fist -
But he was hunched and humbled too.
Stooping beside a manger
Where a baby nuzzled our woollen offerings,
Like an orphaned lamb.

And the woman's touch was gentle.
Approving.
I almost wecomed it.
I was even glad when they left me at her feet.
Couched in rustling straw -
An old lap-dog, learning new tricks.
Someone had to guard the little one,
After all.

And when the time comes,
I shall herd them safely home.
No screeching bird,
No mangy lion,
No rancid fox will bar my way.

As for strangers
With bright swords
And blood on their boots -
It'll be:

"Clear off or I'll open your throats for you,
And no questions asked."

****

THE ANGEL.
****

One Angel, confused by the brightness of stars,
Became lost in time and space
And landed in a High Street
Not far from now.

There were no camels on the sloping pavement,
But the shops glittered like Herod's Castle...
And everywhere people rushed and bustled
With armfuls of precious gifts.

The Angel followed an excited queue
Which no doubt led
To the coiling warmth of a cattle shed
And a nest of hay.
But music jangled the cold air,
And a voice from the sky announced
That the Grotto was closed,
The Car Park was full.

The crowd swarmed angrily away.
So the Angel, who did not give up easily,
Wandered past bright windows
Where trees held out silver branches,
Until the doorways grew darker, drearier,
And the trail reached a lonely square.

A single lamp shone.
A dog, searching for sheep perhaps,
Whimpered -
While in the cave of the bus shelter
A girl whispered to her baby
And smoothed his downy hair.

Then, at last,
The Angel sang.
****

THE PAGE-BOY'S POEM.
****

When first we began, I was happy,
Dressed up in my tunic of gold -
For none of the slaves who were chosen
Would ever be beaten. Or sold.

But sunlight beat down without pity,
The moon froze my blood to the bone;
My days became longer than nightmares,
My dreams were forever of home...
I would wake in the night, cold and shaken,
Lost and bewildered again -
Too old now to weep for my mother,
Too young to sit up with the men.

The trail led us endlessly onward
Through wilderness, valley and town -
Until we arrived at a city
Where bodyguards handed me down.

I cradled the glittering chalice
And followed my Master alone -
Together we swept past the portals,
Together we knelt at the throne.
But Herod was brooding and angry,
Too shocked by our story to speak...
And though his rage flared like a furnace,
His eyes remained fearful and weak...

We calmed him with silk and with spices,
With caskets of sweet-smelling musk.
Then shook off the grit from our sandals,
And clattered away in the dusk.

We rode on a pathway of silver
That painted the hill-tops with light;
My hopes were as bright as the heavens,
A star banished sorrow and fright.
My Master had come to a stable,
And I, with my tribute so fine
Watched as he honoured the mother,
As poor and as humble as mine.

In homage, I offered the chalice,
I placed the rare gift in her hand -
Her fingers were softer than stockdoves,
While mine had been coarsened with sand.

She lifted her child from the manger,
And drew me in closer to see -
I danced round room to delight him,
Then rested my head on her knee.
I woke to a circle of faces,
A muddle of incense and noise -
The peppery snorting of camels,
The questioning chatter of boys.

And now - I rejoiced for the journey,
The truths I had finally seen -
For I had been blessed by a Baby
And slept at the feet of a Queen.

****

THE THREE WISE WIVES.
****

The three Wise Wives, as Wise Wives will -
Waved good bye and watched until
The camel train was out of sight...
Then sat and grumbled half the night:
"Trust the men to think of gold
And gifts a baby cannot hold.
But what's the use? They won't be told."

Next day, the Wives packed PROPER things -
Then tracked the hoof-prints of the Kings.
(They asked the way in each new town -
So missed King Herod's grumpy frown.)

At last, they reached the stable door,
They saw the caskets in the straw;
They soothed the mother, tired and tense
And choked by fumes and frankincense...
While Joseph sadly sniffed the myrrh.
The Wise Wives chorused: "Cheer up, Sir."

"We bring you shawls, and fluffy toys -
And tiny clothes for tiny boys...
And blankets stitched with camel hair;
And cushions for the mother's chair.
And (since a child's a HUGE expense)
Please keep your gold and frankincense -
But swap the myrrh (which no one needs)
For useful baskets made from reeds,"

With that, the Wives nipped through the hay
And cantered home (the quickest way)
To greet their men with cakes and drinks -
And secret smiles and artful winks.
MORAL:
Behind each King and Wise Adviser -
There stands a Wife who knows she's Wiser!

****

GIFTS FOR THE BABY.
****
(Adult Version)

When Mary came to the stable
She brought the wonder of birth -
The gift of a perfect baby,
A present for all the Earth.

When the Inn-Keeper came to the stable
With straw for the customers' bed -
He brought the baby a welcome
And somewhere to lay his head.
When the old wife came to the stable
To cuddle the new-born son -
She brought the blessing of comfort,
A blanket she'd long-ago spun.

When the children came to the stable
To tickle the tiny boy -
They brought the gift of their laughter,
And they filled the air with their joy.

When the white-doves came to the stable
Their music made Bethlehem ring -
They brought a song for the mother
And lullabies for a King.
When the animals came to the stable
Their voices were gentle and deep -
They brought the gift of their patience,
To soothe the baby to sleep.

When the shepherds came to the stable
To stare at the stranger's child -
They brought the fleeces of friendship,
So soft that the baby smiled.

When the rich men came to the stable
They brought a wealth beyond price -
Gifts for a Lord in his glory,
And a life full of sacrifice.
When the Angel came to the stable
In the deepest hour of the night -
He conjured a dream of darkness,
A future of courage and flight.

When Joseph strode from the stable
To save both his son and his wife -
He gave then his quiet courage,
He gave them the promise of life.

When the donkey was led from the stable
To journey from hardship and loss -
His shoulders were steadfast and sturdy,
And his back bore the sign of a cross.
When Jesus escaped from the stable
The pages of destiny turned -

But still, in the dusk of his childhood,
The bright Star of Bethlehem burned.

****

BABOUSHKA'S LAMENT.
****

(While the Three Wise Men journeyed to Bethlehem.)

I should have gone with them, of course -
The three strangers
On their laden horses,
In search of a mythical King.
Should have left breakfast plates
Piled in a bowl,
The samovar still bubbling,
The crumbs scattered on the table
For the mice and the silverfish.

Should have knotted my scarf
And not cared
That my hair was unbrushed,
My slippers worn to holes,
The hem of my skirt frayed and faded
With old age
Like myself.

Should not have minded
What the neighbours thought -
Or said:
"Some people never learn,
Mark my words she'll end up
Murdered in her bed."

Well, there's no fool like an old fool
And I have been foolish all my life.
Too cautious, too careful,
Too much of the repectable wife -
Too wary of the unknown
To change now.
Too scared of the unexpected
To chase strangers on a crazy journey,
Through the muffling snow.

And I know to my shame
That even if I could turn back time,
Hear their invitation again and again,
My reply would be the same:
"Oh no.
Not me,
Not Baboushka...
I must guard my good name."

****

HEROD'S STORY.
****

Don't give me that look.
The curled lip, the narrow eye,
I know exactly what it means.
So
What would you have done
In my embroidered shoes?
Welcomed the foreign spies
With wide arms
And perfumed towels?
Filled their saddle-bags with wine
And gifts of silk
Fit for a King?

Or should I have trailed behind them
To worship my own Nemesis,
My little assassin?
Sneer if you like,
But you would have scorned me anyway,
If I had placed my crown of pride
On a baby's head.

And don't tell me
I have set the women weeping,
Or searched for scarlet stains
Under my burnished nails.
It comes down to this -
Which would you rather?
Peace or War?
People need a strong leader
What ever you say
And a warrier King beats a jumped-up peasant
Any day.

So don't give me that look.
Hate me. Fear me if you like.
Call me a fiend, a devil;
Batter me with words of iron.
My armour is thick,
And any fool can criticise me.

But please, please,
Don't despise me.

****

A NOVEL NATIVITY.
****

(One wintry day, these three animals were seen
roaming along a road in Kansas.)

A Camel, a Donkey, a Cow
Formed a friendship as frost whispered: "Now!"
They would follow the road
To a township that glowed
And make someone welcome, somehow.

The Camel and Donkey agreed
With the Cow - there were gifts they would need...
Like a bundle of hay
And their warmth, which would say:
"We bring you a comforting deed."

The Trio kept close through the night,
As they clopped down a ribbon of light;
Till they reached an old shed
Where a Ram raised his head
While a Ewe began bleating with fright.

She groaned on the floor, cold as rain,
But the breath of the Beasts soothed her pain -
They calmed her with words
As the song of the birds
Rejoiced for a birth in the lane.

The mother leaned over her child,
While the father gazed down and he smiled -
Their lamb in its nest
Of sweet hay was blessed
By strangers who softly left town.

The Camel, the Donkey, the Cow
Were happy - but weary by now -
So, when they were found
And led back to home-ground,
They dreamed as they leaned on the plough...

A voice sang a joyful refrain
For a miracle hard to explain -
When a new life began
For a Girl and her Man...
While the Beasts warmed her baby again.

****

(The three companions were soon returned to their Rescue Home.)

THE CHRISTMAS WREATH.

(Adult Version)

What will you bring for the Christmas Wreath,
From the shimmering shops
And the wind-blown heath?

"Silver strings for the stars that shine.
Ivy trendrils for love to twine.
Golden chains for an Infant King,
Leaves as bright as an Angel's wing.
Scarlet threads for a royal birth,
Drifting feathers for Peace on Earth.
Sugar-frosting as sweet as hay,
Mistletoe boughs to greet the day.
Milk-white pearls for a Mother's care..."

"Twists of wool for a shepherd's prayer.
Satin ribbons for swaddling bands,
Fragrant cones from a Husband's hands.
Perfume rare as a princely crown,
Whispers soft as a sleeping town.
Painted blooms that will never die,
Holly sharper than Herod's cry!
A message of Hope in words of red
And moss to cushion the baby's head."

From the shimmering shops
And the wind-blown heath -
These will we bring for the Christmas Wreath.

THE CHRISTMAS BABY.
****

When the Christmas baby
Arrived a week too soon
No one was surprised.
The girl was such a frail creature,
Her man pleasant enough
But sleepy-eyed with worry
And the endless search for work.

Someone heard a cry
From the upstairs room -
And ran to tell the news:
"A Christmas child
Over the chip-shop.
Small as a sparrow
And hair the colour of straw."

So the neighbours came with gifts:
Nothing much -
What with the factory closed
And redundancy spreading like a dose of flu'.

The mother, propped against pillows,
Spoke little -
But smiled as she touched the kindly tributes.
A tiny hat wrapped in white tissue.
A second-hand teddy-bear...
A folded blanket, warm with memories:
"It's clean, love, though well used."

Then the travellers arrived,
Bringing their battered van -
With fragrant oils, sticks of incense,
A brass wind-chime to glitter above the baby's head.

"He's called Noel," said the father,
His voice rough with pride.
And in the vinegar-scented air
The child's future shone
Like a shop-window star.

****

ONE STAR.
****

(Adult Version)

One star
Is all it takes.

Just one star,
Escaping from clouds
To paint a ribbon of silver
Along the frail edges
Of winter twigs.

One small shimmer of light
Reaching down
To touch your chilly fingers
With a spark of hope;
A promise of of warmth
At the end of the darkest trail.

One sudden flash,
One wild firework of joy -
Spilling its magic across a world of gloom,
Until,
Like a child wishing for sleigh-bells,
Your own eyes sparkle
And the kindness of Christmas
Glows and flows
In circles of comfort,
Ripples of delight.

Just one star.
May it shine for you
Tonight.

****

Winter Warmers

WINTER WARMERS.
****

In December, Grandad wears
Coats as big as grizzly bears -
Hats as huge as eagles' nests;
Giant jumpers, baggy vests;
Massive slippers, flip, flop, flap...
Stacks of blankets for his lap.

Scarves that dangle to his toes;
Woolly warmers for his nose;
Trousers thick and soft and hairy;
Gloves so large, they're rather scary;
Clothes to keep him snug and warm,
In hail and gale and snow and storm.

And THEN he takes them off again -
Remarking (with a twinge of pain)...
"Silly me -
I live in Spain!"

****

THE JOLLY JUMPER POEM.
****

I bought a Snowman jumper -
With a scarf and a long, pointy nose.
The grin was enjoyed
But the carrot ANNOYED!
And my new winter coat wouldn't close.

I bought an Elf-Suit jumper -
With a hat and a huge pair of ears.
It was pricey and posh,
But it shrunk in the wash...
A mishap I greeted with cheers.

I bought a Fir-Tree jumper -
It had baubles, a star and a fairy.
The lights sort-of blinked
And the fairy - she winked,
So the total effect was quite scary.

I bought a Santa jumper -
But it came in one MASSIVE size;
So when I went out
The neighbours would shout:
"I wonder who ate all the pies!"

I bought a Reindeer jumper -
It jingled and glowed, shiny bright.
Which was fun for a while,
But I soon lost my smile
When it glittered and jangled all night.

I've found a Christmas jumper -
It was sitting alone on a shelf...
It doesn't perform,
But it DOES keep me warm
And I knitted it all by
MYSELF.

****

(For our lovely Crowthorne Knitters.)

THE CHRISTMAS KNITTER.

Last Christmas, I unwrapped a kit
Which taught me to crochet and knit -
I soon caught the bug - When I made a small slug
And a bed-sock which didn't quite fit.

Well, I practised my skills for a week,
Though my efforts made everyone shriek -
My stitches were saggy - My jumpers were baggy,
But my tea-cosies looked rather chic!
After that, I tried cuddly toys -
Vampires and Zombies for boys;
Then Penguins (full size) - Polar bears with odd eyes,
And a Reindeer who made a rude noise.

By now, I'd developed a feel,
So I knitted a whole Christmas meal!
With plain and with purl - There was gravy to swirl
And sprouts that looked awfully real...
In the Craft Tent, one cold winter's night
My carrots caused whoops of delight,
Till a child went and ate - The peas from my plate -
Which left her in knots (rather tight)!

For Advent this year - I've made Kings
And an Angel with sparkly wings.
The Baby's blue hair - Gave the Vicar a scare,
But his wife liked my Santa on strings.
I'll admit, the whole thing's an addiction,
I am needled by constant affliction -
But I'll cast off the pain - Of repetative strain
And next year I'll crochet a Fiction.
There'll be Scrooge, with his money bags full,
And Marley with fetters to pull,

Plus a Spirit to say - "Beware of the day...
You are HOOKED
And entangled by WOOL."

****

BIRD TABLE BLUES.
****
(For Dear Doris.)

In Winter, Grandma feeds the birds
With kindly thoughts
And friendly words...
And biscuit crumbs, and broken baps;
And bacon rinds,
And breakfast scraps...

And plates of freshly buttered toast;
And bags of chips,
And Sunday roast;
And dumplings (huge and hot and steamy);
And home-made pies,
And gravy (creamy)...

And every sort of cheese and bread,
Until each hungry,
Bird is fed...
To BURSTING point, to bitter end -
Until their legs
Begin to bend!

Until they cannot flap or fly,
Until they simply
Want to die!
Until they roll around the floor,
And weakly twitter:
"Stop! No more."

Then Grandma smiles and says:
"Oh good!
I think they're ready
For their Pud!"

****

GARDENING TIPS.
****

In Winter, I grow birds in my garden.
First, I select the most magical seeds, and broadcast them
On frosty grass.
Then, from bent branches, I string coconuts
Ripe with whiteness;
Or crack papery nutshells,
To sprinkle their soft kernels
Over the crust of the earth.

Cages of temptation swing from hooks
To lure each traveller,
Each hungry migrant, the lost souls...
Even a scattering of crumbs
Can spread enchantment.

At last, the lawn sprouts its first brave blooms -
The trees blossom with feathers;
I catch the rainbow glitter of a starling's wing;
The bright flash of a robin,
The dazzle of a nuthatch - as blue and exotic
As any hot-house orchid.

And while I watch,
My small, grey world embroiders itself with singing flowers.
Beaks chatter and peck for grain;
A wild dancer whirls on the snowy air.
Choirs of glossy plumes tumble down
To explore the borders...
Where golden thorns glint and stab
For buried treasure.

In Summer, my garden fades like a ruined cloth,
Left too long in the sun.
The blackbirds forget their songs;
The magpies grow mothy-drab,
And the roses, for all their perfume,
Do not rise to circle the drowsy sky.

I must wait until the spiders weave their silver spells;
Until berries burn scarlet
And the last apples hum with wasps.
Then I shall choose my most potent seeds
And let my garden
Grow.
****

FLIGHT OF FANCY.
****

(For the wonderful Sir Ken Dodd.)

Today, there's magic in the air -
The oak tree shakes his tangled hair
To spill his golden treasures where...

The frost has painted pathways white,
And in the ivy, diamond bright
The spider webs are strung with light.

And all that morning, wonders grew -
The sky became a field of blue
Where birds, like summer flowers grew.

The willow tree bent low to greet
The grasses dancing at her feet;
And Winter sang a song so sweet...

I saw, between the holly leaves,
How every scarlet berry weaves
A spell my hopeful heart believes.

And now, the fiery Sun sinks down
To gild the rooftops of the town,
While Evening whirls her starry gown...

Today was magical. And rare.
And I should know -
For I was there.

****

SNOW TIME!
****

Roll up now! Roll up! This is Nature's Big Show -
Look out of your window
With eyes all aglow...
There are feathery flakes
Softly drifting - let's go!
Race down the staircase to welcome the SNOW.

Pull on your boots and your bright woolly hat,
Wrap yourself warm
As a squirrel or cat.
Run with the other
While snowballs go SPLAT!
Then build a great boulder - a Snowman wants that.

Pat him with shovels and give him a smile,
Add twiggy fingers
Plus buttons with style.
A carrot for sniffing...
And in a short while
A holly-leaf crown from a shivery pile.

Now you see sledges that slither and swoop.
They skid down the slopes
With a crash and a whoop!
Some children scream,
Some circle and loop -
While three little dogs want to slide with the group.

But soon you grow hungry - it's time for a snack.
You sigh as you follow
The rest of the pack -
You grab a quick bite
From a comforting stack...
But the snow is still calling - still calling you back.

****

SNOW PROBLEM.
****

For Dolphin School.

(One lone, frozen teacher always finds it's their day to be on playground duty.)

Why is it always MY turn to go
Outside? On duty. Whenever there's snow?
I'm here again. Freezing. While wild breezes blow.

The children are shaking the frost from a tree,
Or throwing fat snowballs - and mostly at ME,
When everyone else is indoors. Sipping tea.

The air's growing icy. The wind starts to bite.
The girls start to grumble. The boys start to fight...
I'm covered in snowflakes. My bobble-hat's white.

But look! Past that snowman - a glimpse of the sun,
As a child tugs my sleeve, to say: "Isn't this FUN!"
And suddenly, somehow, I'm glad I'm the one...

Who's standing outside, where the world seems to shine,
Where magical cobwebs, like tinsel entwine -
The Staff Room is boring.
The Playground is MINE!

****

AFTER THE SNOW.
****

(I borrowed this friendly idea from a Vicar on Radio Four.)

This morning, as I trudged the path
Where muddy trickles ran -
I spied a heap of lumps and bumps
That used to be a man...

I found his frosty carrot;
The hat he'd worn with style;
His twiggy hands - and best of all,
His happy Snowman Smile.

****

All my friends have many things
Too dear for me to buy;
Some are really talented -
But I am small. And shy.

Yet - other people sigh because
The snow is just a pile
Of slush and ice and bits of sticks
Where sculptures stood a while...

But in my secret pocket
Still
I keep my Snowman's Smile.

****

THE LONELIEST SNOWMAN.

(For Readers who are tired of Rhymes.)

The loneliest Snowman in all the world
Stands on a tiny
Island of ice
And sails the winter waves.

Often, blizzards blur his hollow eyes
Until he thinks he sees rainbows
Threading the edges of his frosty home.

Sometimes, he glimpses a far-off ship
Slicing the light and glittering
Like a parcel of stars.
And sometimes a passing sea-bird will rest on his hat
To share the silence
For one precious day.

Once, he saw a young walrus rear up
To gaze at him in wonder,
But perhaps it was only a dream creature
Who flickered across the crystals
Of his half-awake mind.

One golden morning, he knows
His glassy raft will slide him down, down,
To lose his loneliness in the wide warmth
Of the Mother Ocean.

Then,
Somewhere green and deep,
A small fish will shiver its fins, twist
And watch the Snowman's brave smile
Shining
Amongst the friendly gardens of coral.

****

SNOW JOKE.
****

I'm here tonight, campaigning for
A very worthy cause -
To put to rights a dreadful wrong
As old as Santa Claus...

And all because you're picturing
(As blizzards start to blow)
A mighty crowd of jolly MEN
You'll build with all that snow!
You'll rake the stuff and shovel it,
You'll pile it in a heap,
You'll mould it and you'll pat it...
It's enough to make me weep.

You'll add a row of buttons, plus
A carrot and a hat -
Then wonder why I seem annoyed!
What could be wrong with that?
I don't object to twiggy hands,
It's not the nose I hate -
But chauvinistic attitudes
I cannot tolerate.

It's equal opportunities
That Winter seems to lack...
And all because a lump of snow
Can never answer back.
It's time to revolutionise,
It's time there was a choice...
A stack of flakes should have some rights
Although it has no voice.

This might have been a Snow Princess,
A Snow Queen, full of pride...
Instead of just a frozen tramp
With sticks stuck in each side.
Snow Women of the World - UNITE!
Let's liberate the lost,
And let their be a wind of change
To welcome Jenny Frost.

Let's change the face of Winter-Time,
Let Snowmen slink away...
Snow longer can they freeze us out -
Snow Ladies - Join TODAY!

****

THE SNOWY SUFFRAGETTES.

I'm sure you know - Long years ago
Snow Women stood together.
They marched in lines - They brandished signs
In nippy winter weather.

With noisy bands - And twiggy hands
They waved each flag and motto...
"We want our rights - Plus woolly tights,"
They chanted round the Grotto.
Their voices soared - But Santa snored
Till Mother Christmas cried:
"We need to go - And proudly show
We'll join them! Side-by-Side."

Now Santa heard - Each angry word:
The Snowmen get the glory!
But Snowy Girls - With shiny curls
Are missed from song and story.

Their wails were wild - But Santa smiled
And said: "I like your thinking!
Without my Wife - I'm sure my life
Would soon be sadly shrinking."
And so, at last - A law was passed
To make Snow Dreams come true...
When blizzards blew - Snow-Women knew
They'd smile at me. And you.

So that is why - Snow PERSONS fly
Together, hand in hand...
And when it's cold - A tale is told
Of Icy Queens who stand
With silver crowns - Instead of frowns,
Across that frosty Land.

SONG OF A CAT WHO HAS JUST DISCOVERED SNOW.
****

(For Merlin.)

Beyond my doorway
Lies an insane, silent universe.
A shivering nightmare
Of frozen wetness.

Someone has buried my world
Beneath a vast, white duvet...
So bright, it stings my sleep-heavy eyes;
So mounded, I sense an invasion of spies...

What lunatic joke is this?
What trick of a diseased mind?

I shall return and yowl my anger -
Punish the humans with claws of wrath...

Now!
I shall punish the fools
Who test my patience.
I shall dry my drenched fur
On their scratched skin -

For my proud tail is chilled
To its frosty bone,
And I do not intend to suffer
Alone.

****

A SHIVER OF WINGS.

The snow was unexpected and duvet-deep,
After winters of drizzle;
Yet the plump flower-beds were soon smudged
And creased
By a tumble of thrushes.

All morning, they patterned the garden with their graffiti
Scribbled footprints on clean sheets
Or stabbed pillows of frost
To steal the last, sunken scraps.

Later,
As we scraped a grubby trail from street to door,
We spied a shiver of wings
Strung along our neighbours' wall.

And there,
Where a garland of scarlet berries once blazed -
The Thrushes clung,
Fieldfare and Redwing
Crammed with ripeness,
To shimmer like a coverlet
Of shaken silk.

WHEREVER DID ALL THE WHITE CHRISTMASES GO?
****

Wherever did all the White Christmases go?
Those mystic confections of spun-sugar snow?
Where are the flakes that should pepper the sky?
The shrieks of the ice-skaters hurtling by?

Where are the sleighs with their tinkling bells?
Where are the frosts on the hedges and fells?
Where are the ghostly, mysterious mounds...
To thrill us with shapes, and to muffle our sounds?

Where are the children with gloves of red wool?
The stacks of fat snowballs, the sledges to pull?
Where are they now, and where were they ever?
A Peter-Pan dream from a Land Never-Never?

A feverish storm in a song-writer's brain?
A cloak of illusions to smother the rain?
The dark, muddy puddles - the clouds low and grey!
The dismal Decembers that haunt us today!
SO
Come back, Mister Crosby - we need you again
To restore a lost world
With your teasing refrain.

****

A THANK YOU NOTE.
****

(A Poem For Our Wonderful N.H.S.)

They're always here to help us when
Our lives have lurched askew -
Surgeons with their super-skills
Who make our hopes come true;
People who push wheelchairs
Round the wards - the whole year through.

Those who love to welcome
Brand new babies to our world;
Those who watch in humming rooms
Where tiny lives are curled;
Those who comfort while we wait
As fate becomes unfurled.

Those with friendly faces
Who are there to meet and greet;
Those who heal the broken, then
Make sure they find their feet;
Those who feed the lonely souls
With kindness, warm and sweet.

Those who see, on clever screens
The workings of the brain;
Those who know the perfect pill
To ease a bitter pain;
Those who bathe the sleepers
Who will never wake again.

Those who wage a constant war
On mites and mess and grime;
Those who care for victims
Of an accident or crime;
Those who work, without complaint,
However late the time.

And those who simply listen
When the words are hard to say -
For ALL of them have vital tasks
And vital roles to play...
So now - let's thank each one of them
Today
And every day.

****

THE CHRISTMAS HEROES.
****

Let's hear it for Heroes
We struggle to name,
Who seldom win medals - Or fortune. Or fame.
The ones we rely on
To serve with a smile,
Who always seem willing - To walk one more mile.

The Cleaners, the Menders
Who put the World right.
The wonderful Carers - Who watch through the night.
The Doctors and Nurses
Who all do their best
To comfort and cure - When we're scared. Or distressed.

The Shop Girls, the Stackers
Who fill up the shelves.
The Marathon Runners - Who dress up as Elves!
The Charity Workers
Who wait half the day
For one single coin - Or a kindly: "Good Day."

The Teachers who patiently
Try to explain,
And when we are stuck - Try again and again.
The Cooks and the Waiters
Who labour away
To please us and feed us - For very small pay.

The People who bring us
Our parcels and post;
The Folk we don't notice - Who help us the most.
The Bin-Men who work
In the wind and the rain.
The Givers of Time - Who will never complain.

The Friends who will listen
When life's going wrong;
The Souls who are Christmassy - All the year long;
Who lift up our hearts
With a smile or a song.
Let's hear it for Heroes - Unsung, yet their worth
Is greater than gold...
They're the Salt of the Earth.

****

DECEMBER DILEMMA.
****

Strange things are happening
All down our street -
The bad-tempered people we constantly meet
Are suddenly smiling!
Whatever's gone wrong?
Our mean Traffic Warden is humming a song.
The girl in the Cafe,
Who always wears black
Is dressed in a scarlet and sparkly mac.

The Man on the bus
With a permanent frown
Is waving at strangers all over the town!
The Bin-Men who CLATTER
And clutter my garden
Are tidy! And quiet! They say: "Beg your pardon."
While grumpy old ladies
(Who scowl like a toad)
Are happily helping Boy-Scouts cross the road!

The Banker who keeps
All his cash behind locks
Has just put a cheque in the charity box.
The local Policeman
With blooming great feet...
He told me a joke - then he gave me a sweet!
And now, our M.P. (who is cold and aloof)
Is kissing the babies
And telling the TRUTH!

I wonder what's happened to gloom? And to sorrow?
Ah!
I've just checked the date -
And it's Christmas
TOMORROW.

****

(This poem was for Sir Ken Dodd.)

THE VISITATION.
****

(For Doris.)

Today, I saw an Angel
on the corner of our street!

Admittedly he wore odd socks
and flip-flops on his feet.

But his T-Shirt gleamed as brightly
as the Gates beyond the Sky;

His hair was soft and golden
as he drifted softly by.

His smile was soft and dreamy,
his feathered wings were flappy...

Today
I saw an Angel - on our street!
That's why I'm happy.

****

HERE IS THE NEWS.
****

Here is the News
And somewhere today -
A baby was born.
A team raced away
To rescue the missing, the sad and the stray.

Someone uncovered,
From deep underground
A fabulous creature
That once roamed around...
While the cure for a problem was joyfully found.

Somebody modest
Became, overnight -
A genuine Hero.
A wrong was put right.
There were small deeds of kindness - the gift of delight.

Some lonely people
Felt loved, after all.
The crowds on the pavement
Decided to call
Families, friends - as a hush seemed to fall.

And now they remembered
A custom as old
As firelight and laughter
And moments to hold
In their hearts like a treasure - far richer than gold.

Here is the News -
And somewhere, today,
Good things still happened...

Let's keep it that way.

****

THE CHRISTMAS CONJUROR.

The Christmas Conjuror
Pulls back his starry sleeves
And laces his long, frosty fingers.
Then he blows softly
On his bare knuckle-bones,
Winks at a wide-eyed child
And snap!
From his pale palms
The snowflakes flutter and rise like birds
On the glittering air;
Or whirl around our heads in silent swarms.

Now he claps his crafty hands
Once, twice,
And snatches a silver hair
From his own, cold beard.
Moonlight touches the taut thread
As he twists it, shapes it,
Shakes it like a ribbon of silk...
Until a string of icicles
Decorates the roof, the fence, the bare twigs
Of the apple tree.

At last, he raises his wand
To shower us with magic.
Beneath our feet
The grass is a crystal pathway.
Every hedge wears a necklace of royal webs
And the green pond becomes a mirror
To reflect our wonder.

But when we turn to thank him,
The Christmas Conjuror
Has faded away
Like an echo
Of quiet
Laughter.

****

AN ADVENTUROUS ADVENT

THE ADVENT CALENDAR.
****

On the First of December the Panto is booked;
On the Second, the pudding and cake must be cooked;
On the Third, I'll be choosing a gift for a friend;
On the Fourth, I'll be sorting the cards we must send;
On the Fifth, I'll be searching for names I forgot...
On the Sixth, I'll be ready for mailing the lot.

On the Seventh, I'll queue to buy stamps half the day;
On the Eighth, I'll be hoovering cobwebs away;
On the Ninth and the Tenth, I'll be cleaning some more;
The Eleventh, I'll fix a bright wreath on the door.
On the Twelfth, decorations will have to be hung.
On the Thirteenth, the lights (if they're blinking) are strung.

The Fourteenth, it's time to drag home - a small tree;
The Fifteenth, it's covered covered in tinsel. And me!
On the Sixteenth, I'll cut holly sprigs for the hall;
The Seventeenth, pin all the post on the wall;
The Eighteenth, some presents still have to be found;
The Nineteenth, I'm shopping and tearing around.

The Twentieth, I'll be the quickest of packers;
On day Twenty One, must remember the crackers;
On day Twenty Two, I'll be icing the cake;
On day Twenty Three, I'll have mince pies to bake;
On day Twenty Four, I'll be working non-stop -
With last minute cooking and trips to the shop.

On day Twenty Five, I'll be first out of bed,
Festive and frantic and worn to a shred!
AND
If all has gone well, then maybe. Perhaps -
On day Twenty Six
What I'll do is...
COLLAPSE.
****

AN ADVENTUROUS ADVENT.
****
(For Sir Ken Dodd.)

Good grief! It's boring Advent time -
I'll write myself a list in rhyme...
Day One - Mix pud in tumble-drier.
Day Two - Set paper chains on fire.

Day Three - Tie antlers on the cat.
Day Four - Paint hoof-prints on the mat.
Day Five - Hang spiders from the tree.
Day Six - Set grumpy turkeys free.

Day Seven - Bake a Firework-Pie.
Day Eight - Teach Penguins how to fly.
Day Nine - Build Snowmen round the bed.
Day Ten - Spray all the door-knobs red.

On Day Eleven - Ice the Telly.
Day Twelve - Fill bath with fruit and jelly.
Day Thirteen - Glue the car to skiis.
Day Fourteen - Gift-wrap Stilton cheese.

Day Fifteen - Fuse the fairy lights.
Day Sixteen - Dress the dog in tights.
Day Seventeen - Block sink with cake.
Day Eighteen - Give the drinks a shake.

Day Nineteen - Juggle sprouts and peas.
Day Twenty - Catch a cold and sneeze.
Day Twenty One - To make things jolly,
Decorate the chairs with holly.

Day Twenty Two - Now stuff the bird
With cotton-wool and lemon curd.
Day Twenty Three - Let Grandad doze
Then strap a lightbulb to his nose.

Day Twenty Four - While Granny's rocking,
Pour some custard in her stocking.
Day Twenty Five - When all that's done...
Let's fly away and have some fun.

****

(Please don't try this at home!)

THE CHILDREN'S ADVENT CALENDAR.

(It is an extremely tasteful calendar too - with LOVELY pictures.)

"What's behind the window?
Oh look! It's a TREE!"
(The kids aren't excited -
They leave that to me.)

"What's behind the window?
Oh good! It's a SLEIGH!"
(The kids aren't excited -
They wander away.)

"What's behind the window?
A King! Dressed in GOLD!"
(The kids aren't excited -
This stuff leaves them cold.)

"What's behind the window?
Hooray! It's a CRIB."
(The kids aren't excited -
It's like a damp squib.)

"What's behind the window?
Chocolate. What FUN!"
(The kids ARE excited -
They've swiped it...
And
RUN!)

****

CHRISTMAS CARD QUESTIONNAIRE.
****

Who wants a Cool card?
A Rock-and Rolling Yule card?
A Rapping-Reindeer-Rule Card
Not for me.

Who wants a Cute card?
A Robin-in-a Suit card?
A Cat-in-Santa's-Boot card?
Please not me.

Who wants a Snowy card?
A Glittery-and-Glowy card?
A Blustery and Blowy card?
PLEASE not me.

Who wants a Jolly card?
Pop-out-Sprigs-of-Holly card?
A Squeaky-Singing-Dolly card?
NO! Not me.

Who wants a Rude card?
A Christmassy-yet-Crude card?
A Rudolph-in-the-Nude card?
Not for me!

Who wants a Pretty card?
Snowflakes-with-a-Ditty card?
Jokers-with-a-Witty card?
Just not me.

Who wants a Square card?
A Fluffy-Polar-Bear card?
A Penguin-in-a-Chair card?
Still not me.

Who wants a Red card?
Stockings-round-the-Bed card?
Fairies-on-the-Shed card?
Maybe me?

Who wants a funny card?
Snowmen-on-a-Sunny card?
LOTS of Christmas Money card?
ME! ME! ME!

****

MERRY MAIL?
****

No more cards
And no more stamps,
No more festive writer's cramps.
No more nasty
Tasting glues,
No more stress and no more queues.

No more journeys
In the rain,
To the Box and back again.
No more robins,
No more snow.
No more twinkly Snowmen.
No!

All that silly
Stuff is gone -
This year we are logging-on!
No more bother,
No more fuss,
E-Mail is the thing for us...

One short message,
One quick rhyme -
Signed and sent in record time.
(And if you like
Our words of cheer -
We'll send the same stuff
EVERY YEAR!)

****

A FESTIVE CONFUSION.
****

(For Sir Richard Baker.)

I've picked up the cards from the mat in the hall -
I've sorted and sifted and studied them all...
And most of the senders I I dimly recall -
But THIS one is driving me right up the wall.
Can anyone help me? Does anyone know...
James, Little Jenny,
Young Molly and Mo?

Are they those neighbours from Hastings? Or Hell?
Those distant relations we never knew well?
The waiters who worked at that ghastly Hotel?
I've thought really hard - but they don't ring a bell!
Can anyone place them? Those mystery names?
Mo, Little Jenny,
Young Molly and James.

Or could they be school-friends from ages ago?
That couple who helped when the car wouldn't go?
Those people who borrowed my best garden hoe?
The students we sponsored to hike in the snow?
Can anyone picture this foursome so jolly?
James, Little Jenny,
And Mo and young Molly?

Or maybe we met on some long-distance flight?
Or else, at the airport when nothing went right?
Those terrible tourists who talked half the night?
(I've lost their address - but I'd know them by sight!)
Oh! Give me a clue! I'd be grateful for any...
Mo and young Molly
And James and wee Jenny?

They're driving me crazy, I'm losing my mind!
I'm groping around like the lost or the blind...
I've searched all my lists but there's nothing to find -
Then my wife squints across at the message they've signed:
"Your glasses are steamy. You're looking through fogs...
It's your big sister Jane
And her three stupid dogs."

****

THE CHRISTMAS NEWS BLUES.
****

At Christmas time (it's sad but true)
All the friends you ever knew
Plus all your long-lost family too
Will send their latest News to you.
News you didn't want to know.
News that makes your life seem slow.
News that fills your heart with woe -
News that makes depression grow...

Here's a note from Cousin Bea -
Her husband's won the Lottery!
And Little Kate who's only three
Has gained a First-Class Maths Degree.

Now some lines from Jim and Jane:
Who find the Winter SUCH a pain -
They're cruising round the World again,
Then setting off to live in Spain.

Amanda's sent a long report -
Her son's become a whizz at Sport!
He's never beaten. Never caught..
The BEST his trainer's ever taught.

Remember dear old Ted from school,
Who used to joke and act the fool?
He's changed his name to Mister Cool
And lives a life that makes you drool.

And even Rose, who used to be
Just as sad as you and me...
Has learned to sing - and suddenly
She's hosting shows on ITV.

****

As for us - the dog has died;
The cat's left home, the children cried.
The roof has leaked, the holes gape wide -
The house (we're told) will soon subside.
There's only one thing left to do -
We'll write a page of news to YOU!
To say we're rich and clever too -
(With any luck - it might come true)!

****

SANTA'S CHRISTMAS NEWS BLUES.
****

One winter, dear Old Santa
Found some cards upon his mat -
Most of them weighed half a ton - and all of them were fat.
So - were they full of catalogues for cosy boots or shoes?
Or long and greedy wish-lists?
No! They bulged with Christmas News.

The first was from the Fairy,
So it twinkled merrily:
'I've had a simply magic month. I'm proud as I can be.
The Twitter Vote has sent me to
The Top of This Year's Tree.'

The Snowman's note was boastful -
'I am pleased to let you know
I'm the finest and the fittest of 'The Persons Made Of Snow.'
I've even won the Snowball Fight -
Just watch my Fan-Club grow.'

More bragging came from Rudolph,
(The deer who brightly glows):
'I'm the fastest of the Fliers - as that Sat-Nav woman knows...
I've raced against the rockets
And I beat them by a nose!'

The Penguin was the neatest,
While the Elf was twice as clever
As any other Character in any Contest EVER!
While the Gnomes who paint the presents
Wrote: 'Can Robots beat us? NEVER!'

Old Santa read the letters
And he gave a weary groan -
Then he sent his Christmas cards and wrote a message of his own:
'I'm sure your year was just like mine - It had its Ups and Downs -
Its worries and its wonders,
Its days of smiles and frowns...
SO
You don't need to impress me, or convince me you're a Star!
Because, you see - I like you
Just exactly as you are.

****

ALL LIT UP.
****

I'm not a grumpy person
(As all my neighbours know)
But irritating house-lights - this Christmas have to GO!

The first year, there were tasteful loops
That dangled from the trees
Like icicles or tiny stars - effects designed to please.

The next year, there were coloured bulbs
In rainbows round the door -
Or twisted up the aerial - but that's what lights are for.

The third year, there was Santa
In his jolly beard and hat
Appearing from the chimney-pot - there's no excuse for that!

The fourth year, Herds of Reindeer
Were prancing on the tiles,
While Rudolph's nose flicked on and off - and lit the sky for miles.

The fifth year, there were Snowmen
Who glowed beside the gate.
They glared at passing strangers - with frosty frowns of hate.

The sixth year, Bears and Robins
Were waving from the Sleigh,
With blinking eyes and sing-songs - that tinkled night and day.

The strobe effects were torture,
The flashing Gnomes were rude -
And the constant stream of Tourists - did NOT improve the mood.

Spectators came in taxis
In coaches and on bikes,
With crowds of noisy children - and Carols sung on mikes!

We couldn't sleep last Christmas,
We couldn't rest at all...
The wretched lights were dancing - across the bedroom wall.

I'm not a grumpy person,
I'm fond of festive cheer -
But the neighbours made me promise...
TO SCRAP MY LIGHTS THIS YEAR!

****

CANDLE COMPLAINT.
****

Our house is stacked with candles
And each year - we're given more.
(Though we haven't had a power-cut since 1994).

Yet still the things keep coming,
In a range of shapes and sizes -
Some as large as Totem Poles. (Oh, how we love surprises).

Some are lumpy Snowmen,
Some are whimsical and sweet,
Some are wide-eyed Penguins with distressing, drippy feet.

Some are just like oranges
With dimples and a wick -
And here's a ripe banana. Please don't bite it. You'll be sick.

Some have metal gadgets
Which revolve and rattle bells.
Some are green. Or scarlet. But they ALL make awful smells.

Some have cut-out windows
Where a picture seems to dance,
But will we ever light them? Or unwrap them? Not a chance.

Candles, frankly, aren't a gift
Our Christmas table lacks -
We don't need fumes in all the rooms, or blobs of molten wax.

So, if our roof starts blazing
With a fierce and spicy flame -
Don't search for signs of lightning, or an arsonist to blame...

Don't curse our faulty fuse box
When the Firemen come to save us -
The cause of all our woes will be
The candles that YOU gave us!

****

CHRISTMAS LIGHTS.
****

There's a garland of lights in the ivy,
There are shimmering stars by the score;
There are torches to gleam
In a long, silver stream
When you follow the path
To my door.

There's a lantern that waits in the hallway,
With a flame that stands tall and alone;
There are candles to glow
In a flickering row
By my window, to welcome you
Home.

There are golden cascades in the fir tree -
But the light I am longing to see
Is the spark of surprise
That will shine in your eyes
When you open your present
From Me.

****

THE CHRISTMAS FAIRY-LIGHTS.
****

Down would come the plastic tree
Out of the loft
And alongside it -
On the needle-free carpet
We would carefully, carefully place
The dreaded shoe-box.

Then,
While we straightened the branches
With crossed fingers
And tied tongues -
Dad would lift the lid.

"The Lights!" he would cry
In a voice full of pride and expectation.
"Here we go!"
How come he didn't remember?
How come he didn't know?

We knew
Because it happened every year...

And an hour later
An angry, hot, glaring, swearing, long torture later...
We would still be searching for
The one rotten bulb
That decided to
BLOW!

****

(Three Quick Christmas Carols.)

IN THE WET MIDWINTER.
****

(To be sung to the tune of: In The Bleak Midwinter.)

In the wet Midwinter
Poor old Granny moans:
"I've got leaky wellies,
I've got creaky bones.
Water swirls around my bed
Where my slippers float -
All I want for Christmas
Is a Motor Boat."
****

A JOLLY JINGLE.
****

(To be sung to the tune of: 'Jingle Bells'.)

Aches and pains. Icy rains -
Winter's here again -
Fingers blue and festive flu'
And brussels-sprouts to drain...
Ooooh!
Noses run. Oh what fun
Christmas colds can be -
Santa Claus should visit us
In JUNE if you ask me.
****

FA, LA, LA, LA, LA...
****

(To be sung to the tune of: 'Deck The Halls..')

'Tis the season to be busy,
Decorate the tree and paint the star;
Race around until you're dizzy,
Cram a thousand things inside the car.
Every year we stagger through it -
Flap-a-lot. Wrap-a-lot. Sign our name...
Who can tell us why we do it?
We have only got - ourselves to blame.

****

THE CAROL SINGER'S STORY.
****

I thought it was: 'Good King Wences'.
That's how it seemed to me...
'Good King Wences LAST looked out -
Obviously.

Perhaps he was feeling dizzy,
Perhaps he was sick of the snow.
Perhaps he'd lost his spectacles -
We'll never know,

Perhaps I should say I'm sorry,
But 'Wences' just sounds fine...
So
You can sing your boring words
And I'll sing MINE.

****

HARK THE HORRID.
****

(To the tune of: 'Hark The Herald'.)

Hark! The horrid Musak sing-ings:
Jingle Bells and Five Gold Rings.
When the torture starts agai-ain,
Ear-worms jangle in your brain...
Slade and Rudolph keep on coming -
Flying Snowmen won't stop humming...
Rocking Robins make you scream,
Frosty-ee haunts your darkest dream.
Hark! The merry Musak clangs
While your-or Christmas Head-ache
BANGS.

****

ONE MORE TIME FOR ME.
****

I don't object to 'Deck The Halls',
Or 'Rocking Round The Tree' -
I'm not against 'O Little Town'
Or faithful: 'Come All Ye'.

I don't complain at 'Frosty'
Or Rudolph's flashy nose,
Or 'Wenceslas' or 'Figgy Pud' -
I'm quite prepared for those.
I'm really not the awkward sort -
You hum it and I'll play...
If only we could scrap ONE song
My temper wouldn't fray.

It isn't 'Ding, Dong, Merrily'
That makes me dread the date.
It isn't Bing with Christmas snow -
It's 'Jingle Bells' I hate!
It's not the tune. It's not the notes.
(You warble like the birds)
The thing that drives me round the bend -
Is:
NO ONE KNOWS THE WORDS!

You start all right, with 'Oh What Joy',
The bits you learned from Mum...
But after 'Dashing through the snow'
You start your tum-tee-tum!'
Now, 'Pom-te-pom' and 'Dum-de-dee'
Are not what maestros like -
No wonder that I slam my lid
And say - "I'll go on strike!"
So
If you want my sharps and flats -

Choose something else to sing...
Or else - go home and learn the lines,
And make my Sleigh-Bells ring!

****

DECEMBER SONG.
****

What will it be? Our December Song?
The one that we all want to buy?
The jingly, tingly, sing-along-song
With a voice that's incredibly high.

We'll hear it in the morning - We'll hear it in the dark,
We'll hear it in the kitchen and we'll hear it in the park.

What will it be? Our December Song?
The one we constantly play?
The dreamy-beat, sugar-sweet, Christmassy tune
That haunts us all night and all day?

We'll hear it in the playground - We'll hear it in the car,
We'll hear it in the chip shop - And the Charity Bazaar.

What will it be? Our December Song?
The one that we start to despise!
The jolliest, holliest, rock-and-roll rap -
That puts a mad gleam in our eyes.

We'll hear it in the High Street - We'll hear it in the store,
We'll hear it in the bathroom - Even though we lock the door!

What will it be? Our December Song?
The one that induces despair?
The mangled and tangled and jangly tune
That tempts us to tear out our hair!

We'll hear it in the our nightmares - We'll hear it in our dreams,
We'll hear it deep inside our minds
Till everybody
SCREAMS!

****

BAH HUMBUG!
****

Don't say I'm a Scrooge or a spoiler of fun -
It's just that the Seasonal Songs have begun!

I don't mind a Carol that's sung by a Choir
With mittens and lanterns and groups round the fire.
I don't mind the children who thump on my door,
Then mumble one chorus - no less and no more...

It's good to be rocking around a bright tree
With friends and good neighbours - that's how it should be!

But what makes me moody and gloomy and glum -
Is the wall-to-wall MUSAK now Advent has come.
It jingles and tinkles with never a pause -
It warbles a story of Old Santa Claus...

Or a fat, creepy snowman or snowflakes and stuff
And nobody dares to scream: "Stop! That's ENOUGH!"

It rattles my brain while I'm choosing a gift,
It drones from the phones and it lurks in the lift.
It winds up my mind like a mad clockwork toy,
It drives me to tears and deprives me of joy!

I snarl at the Shop Girl, I glare at an Elf;
I growl at the cuddly Bears on the shelf -

I stagger back home with no presents to give,
No cards and no paper - and no will to live!
I close all my windows. I shudder and moan -
Then I spend Christmas Day in a cupboard - alone.
BUT
At least, there's no MUSAK to ruin my tea -
Just darkness. And spiders. And silence...
And Me.

****

MUSIC HATH CHARMS.
****

They gave us -

Musical doormats. Musical ties.
Musical cushions (now there's a surprise).

Musical candles. Musical socks.
Musical pants in a Musical Box.

Musical movies and Musical books;
A Musical toaster for Musical cooks.

Musical Snowmen and Musical trees -
(They give you a scare if you suddenly sneeze.)

Musical teddies and Musical toys,
A Musical goblet - that simply annoys!

Music so ghastly - it makes people weep -
Music that ruins your life and your sleep.

Music that fills you
With dread and despair...
But me? I'm tone deaf,
So I really
DON'T CARE!

****

(At last - a proper Choir for Christmas and the N.H.S.)

SWEET SINGING IN THE CHOIR.
****
(For Sir Ken Dodd.)

Here's a soprano whose voice is so sweet,
Whose hair is so tidy, whose blouse is so neat -
Who seems rather prim, but who wiggles her feet
In cosy old slippers tucked under her seat.

Here is a choirboy who craftily chose
To sit at the back in the dimly-lit rows.
His mouth, like a cherub's, will open and close
But he's texting his girlfriend and EVERYONE knows!

Here's a contralto who warbles with zest,
But sings in a different key from the rest!
She's terribly sorry and terribly stressed,
So she's miming her lines (which is all for the best).

Here is a tenor who croaks like a crow.
He chokes on his cough-sweet, his nose starts to glow.
He lines up his tissues for blow after blow
And his musical sneezes are stealing the show!

Here are the baritones, steady and strong -
And here are the basses who rumble along -
They're loud and they're proud and although they go wrong
They'll be shaking the spire by the end of the song.

Here's the conductor, who's wearing a frown.
His eyebrows shoot up as his baton swoops down.
He glares like a tyrant, he swishes his gown -
But we know he's the kindliest man in the town.

And here are the people we love and admire -
Whose hearts are as warm as a flickering fire;
Whose voices (though weary) soar higher and higher -
Our seasonal heroes -
Our own Christmas Choir.

****

.MERRY MUSAK.
****

Old Santa has an i-pod now -
So when he packs the toys,
His sack is stuffed with parcels
And his ears are stuffed with noise.

Now - take a risk and place your bets
On tunes for his Top Ten -
But if you've chosen 'Silent Night'
You'd better guess again!

Did Santa download Christmas hits
By Bing? Or Cliff? Or Slade?
Or did he go for 'Jingle Bells'?
You're failing, I'm afraid.
And as for boughs of holly
Or the running of the deer,
Or drummer boys, or donkeys,
Or King Wenceslas - no fear!

Perhaps he's fond of 'Auld Lang Syne',
Or Frosty in the snow?
Or sexy 'Santa-Baby',
Or that barn where North Winds blow?
Or Mummy with her mistletoe?
Or Rudolph with his nose?
Or a Pear-Tree with a Partridge?
Oh, bad luck! It's none of those.

No - Santa bungs his earphones in,
And flies to far-off lands
While Rocking to the Cool-Yule-Beat
Of
Heavy Metal Bands.

****

AWAY FROM IT ALL.
****

We went away last Christmas - a Hotel by the sea,
With every kind of comfort - plus cocktails round the tree,
And crackers with our cornflakes...
Our dinner and our tea.

We each had little presents - beside our breakfast tray -
For Him, a tie and hanky - we later gave away!
For Her - some foreign perfume
(Which lasted one whole day).

The food was simply splendid - Nouvelle and Cordon Blue,
Arranged in pretty patterns - not quite our taste, it's true,
But that's the price you pay for
No washing-up to do.

At supper, there were carols - recorded by a choir,
Then party games and quizzes - with strangers round the fire,
Who all wore smart, new outfits
(Though ours were just on hire).

We had a lovely Christmas - We really can't complain,
The manager was charming - and he said to come again...
But Boxing day, quite early,
We set off for the train.

****

This year, we'll have muddle and panic and noise -
And sinkfuls of saucepans
And rooms full of toys,...
And a real, homely Christmas
With REAL homely joys.

****

DEAR OLD DECORATIONS

CHRISTMAS TREE CAT.

The cat up the tree
Is confused as can be -
By tinsel that traps the unwary.

Then the pot starts to sway
In a worrying way
Till her yowls are incredibly scary.

Our star has been scragged.
And the branches have sagged,
The lovely glass baubles are hairy...

While the lightbulbs go POP
As she clings to the top -
BUT
At least it's a change
From the Fairy!

THE CHRISTMAS TREE FAIRY.
****

I'm certain our Christmas Tree Fairy is wearing a squinty-eyed look -
Just because, this year she's wonky
And spinning around on her hook.

Just because Dribble (our poodle) decided to give her a wash.
Just because Uncle enhanced her
With spots and a felt-pen moustache.

Just because someone has borrowed (and buckled) her twinkly wand;
Just because somebody floated
Her cute little crown on the pond.

Just because one person dyed her - so now she looks just like a Goth.
Just because something has chewed her -
The hamster perhaps? Or a moth?

Just because one useless lightbulb EXPLODED and shredded her frock.
Just because Gran made a new one
Recycled from Grandad's old sock.

Just because Aunty was clumsy and wiggled her wig out of place.
Just because Dad shook the Snow-Spray
Which splattered her wings. And her face.

Just because eight plastic Reindeer have stabbed
her with antlers all night.
Just because Mum sort-of fainted
And said that she gave her a fright.

Just because one little candle has melted her shoes.
And her feet...
But WHY does she look so aggressive?
She used to be EVER so sweet.

****

THE FAIRY IN THE LOFT.
****

In a box that's gone soft - I've been left in the loft,
So sometimes I feel I'm forgotten.
But the moths in my sock
Have embroidered my frock
With delicate holes in the cotton.

My wings have come loose - (they were never much use),
But the Bat says they're fine as they are;
And the Spiders are fond
Of my bendy old wand -
They can bungee-jump straight off my star.

In my small, silver shoes - the Mice like to snooze -
They're smelly but eager to please.
And if I feel sad
Life isn't so bad
When they squeak happy songs round my knees.

My tinsel was knotted - until a Rat spotted
The problem and gave it a chew.
And when I'm afraid
That my magic might fade -
He whispers: "Your dreams will come true."

That's when I remember - my first, fine December -
The glitter of gifts far below.
But I love my new friends,
So if Santa Claus sends
A tree, just for me - I will GLOW!

Now my lid gently raises - a bulb brightly blazes!
"Here she is!" someone laughs: "She's so sweet -
With some sparkle and glue
Plus a sticker or two
She'll soon make our Christmas complete."

Now I'm free, look at me - at the top of my tree
Shiny new, with the world at my feet,
And when Christmas is done
I'll have plenty of fun
With my friends in the loft - What a treat!

****

I'M DREAMING OF A GREEN CHRISTMAS.
****

SO...
Out goes the tinsel,
The glitter, the tree -
It's all artificial and ghastly to see.
We'll ditch decorations
And plasticky toys;
The flashy, fake Santa who makes a rude noise.

The bright, blow-up Snowman
Who sags at our door;
The faded old wreath dropping dust on the floor.
And as for the Fairy -
Her wig's come undone,
But
Our house looks so dismal. No colour. No fun.

Then Gran, with a giggle says:
"Come out to play...
We'll find proper holly, in hedgerows. Hooray!
We'll plant a small fir tree
Then bring it inside,
To sit by our window and rustle with pride."

"We'll clip paper stars
To each branch till they shine,
We'll add scarlet berries - and ivy to twine."
The air becomes spicy -
And Gran says: "You'll see...
Each year, you'll grow taller - and so will your tree!"

"Now look! On the doormat
The Christmas Cards fall -
We'll have Robins and Reindeer to hang on the wall..."
While the games Granny shares
Are too daft to be true!
SO
We love our GREEN Christmas -
And you'll love yours too.

****

(But of course - some of us are wishing for Snow...)

SNOWFLAKES.
****

There are snowflakes made from paper
On each window and each wall;
There are snowflakes in the kitchen
In the bathroom and the hall.

There are snowflakes in our bedrooms;
On each cupboard and each door;
There are snowflakes (slightly trampled)
On the carpets and the floor.

There are snowflakes hung from ribbons
To annoy us on the stairs;
There are snowflakes painted silver,
On our doorways and our chairs.

There are snowflakes on our ceiling;
There are snowflakes on the tree;
There are snowflakes (large and little)
In every place I see...

There are snowflakes in a blizzard
Every place those flakes can go!
There are FAR too many snowflakes
But -
There isn't any
SNOW!

****

THE BAY TREE.
****

Your sky-rocket trees
Bought from heaps on the ground,
Are tall, proud and pointy...
But OUR tree is round.

It lives on our lawn in a pot of red clay,
Not a Pine, nor a Fir - our tree is a Bay.

It stands in the sun,
Or the rain if it pours...
But just before Christmas
Our tree comes indoors.

A circular tree on a lollipop stick...
And though it sounds silly - our tree does the trick.

We drape its green leaves
In a silver disguise,
And though it seems crazy
Our tree takes the prize!

We paper the pot and we tie a red bow,
And though it sounds foolish - our tree seems to know.

It watches our fun,
And whatever we do -
The day feels complete
When our tree is here too.

But after Twelfth Night (if there's rain, hail or snow)
The Party is over. Our Tree has to go...

We strip off the stars,
Let the snowflakes unweave;
Then take down the baubles -
Our tree has to leave...

It looks through our shivery window all day -
But what it is thinking
Our tree will not say.

****

(A Bay Tree never grows too tall - and it doesn't
leave needles to spike your toes.)

POT PLANT PROBLEM.
****

We bought a Poinsettia,
A brilliant red -
To brighten our Christmas -
That's what the pot said.

But now it's gone droopy
And brown to distract us...
Next year, we'll have sense
And we'll stick with a Cactus.

****

OUR BEAUTIFUL POT PLANT.
****

It's tall. It's exotic.
It's wondrous and bright.
It stands on our table -
A gift to delight.

The family gasps at
Our lovely display -
So fragrant. So festive,
A triumph they say.

A pity, they tell us -
One day they will droop.
Those petals will shiver
And splatter your soup.
SO
Nobody tells them
Our pot-plant LOOKS dear!
But it's all artificial...
AND
It'll come back
Next year.

****

OUR CRAZY CHRISTMAS.
****
(Lock-Down - Summer 2021.)

Our lives felt so boring, we all heaved a sigh -
Then somebody said: "Let's give Christmas a try."
For no special reason. We didn't know why...

But the days were so dreary, our hopes hit the wall.
So we ransacked the loft. Hung a star in the hall,
While Dad (wearing antlers) threw sweets at us all!

We dangled our garlands of holly-leaves (fake);
There were cards to be crafted; a Grotto to make,
As Mum perched a penguin on top of a cake.

We couldn't find crackers to rattle or flap,
But we told silly jokes and we all shouted 'SNAP'!
Then we sang happy songs so our Granny could clap.

The pot-plants wore tinfoil; the puppy wore wings;
We wrapped empty boxes with ribbons and strings,
And we acted a play about camels and kings.

We sat round a bonfire of red-paper flames -
We tried to guess film-stars and world famous names;
Then we all got the giggles; invented daft games...

When, suddenly, somehow, without any snow,
We all heard a jingle, a merry: "HO! HO!"
We gazed at each other. The room seemed to glow -

Our house was still dusty. Our paintings still wet.
There weren't any glittering tables to set,
Or huge heaps of presents. Or riches -
And yet
That was the Christmas
We'll never forget.

****

THE BIRD IN THE TREE.
****

(A true story - in Ellon, Aberdeenshire, 2021.)

Far away in Scotland where the days are dark, I'm told -
Where squirrels wrap their furry tails
Like scarves to beat the cold...
The people huddle close at home, to wear a festive smile -
And just like you, they find a tree
To decorate with style.

Outside, the little creatures will be hiding from the blast;
They try to forage scraps of bread,
Then scamper hard and fast.
And even owls and mighty birds will shiver in the snow -
They'll hunt for tiny shrews and mice
While whirl-winds wildly blow.

But look! A rather handsome bird has spotted branches brave!
She spies an open window - so
She swoops inside a cave!
A space without a dripping wall - No bats. No smell of moulds.
Instead a world so cosy warm
A wondrous world unfolds.

Above her head are starry lights, that twinkle like the moon;
The fir tree seems to call to her:
"You're safe. You'll sleep quite soon."
At once, she settles on a branch - so bright it's like a dream...
She's dry at last and drowsy
While her feathers softly gleam.

Next morning, someone notices an Angel that can fly!
The phone is rung. The experts come -
Although she wonders why?
She whirls away at break of day - a happy Sparrow Hawk!
She won't forget those glinting stars,
But if she could - she'd talk...

While all the laughing rescuers drink mugs of warming tea -
"It makes a change from Partridges -
And Doves inside a Tree."

****

WE WISH YOU A THRIFTY CHRISTMAS.
****
(Our Motto - 'Make Do And Mend'.)

This year, our gifts are all home-made,
Like daft Blue Peter projects.
So socks and sticks and bits of string are now quite useful objects.

We've built a shiny Christmas tree
From rusty nails and springs -
Our Fairy is a yoghurt pot with toilet-paper wings.

The heating's off, the fire's gone out -
We huddle round a candle.
We sip some luke-warm water from a mug without a handle.

While even Santa feels the pinch -
His boots are tight and leaky.
The moths have munched his trousers, so he's damp and cold and creaky.

He can't afford expensive oats
To feed his Reindeer Crew -
They'll just have HALF a carrot each, and no mince pies to chew.

I'm told his Wife is frosty too!
She wrote her list with love...
She asked for something new to wear - she got an Oven Glove.

And as for us, we're sitting here.
No treats. No cakes. No jelly.
There's just a boring Antiques Show, that's popped up on the telly.

But wait a minute! Don't despair -
That broken mug we HATE...
They say it's worth a fortune! Grab your coats...
Let's CELEBRATE.

****

THE WRAPPING PAPER WRAP.

Well, you choose a gift
And you choose a ball
Of expensive string from a festive stall;
And a fancy bow
At a fancy price;
And a glitter-kit for some stick-on-ice.

And a snowman tag,
And a silver pen,
And some shiny tape costing Five Pound Ten!
And a paper roll
In a bright design
With a row of bears in a cheerful line.

And you pay the bill
And you scurry back,
And you clear a space and you start to pack...
But the piece you snip
Is a bit too small,
And the string's too long and the scissors fall!

And the ends won't meet
Though you try and try,
And the wretched bears seem about to cry...
So you hold the stuff
With your teeth and knees,
Then the glitter spills so you start to sneeze.

Now the tape gets stuck
On the stupid floor,
And the stupid string tangles more and more
And the stupid gift
Is a stupid shape,
And there's dust and fluff on the stupid tape -

And the paper rips,
And your spirits sag -
So you bung the lot in a paper bag.

****

THE PERFECT PRESENT WRAPPER.

I'm a Christmas-Present Wrapper,
I'm a Rapper who can Wrap -
So when the people see my skills
They stare and cheer and clap.

I can wrap a Rudolph Reindeer;
I can wrap a tiny box;
I can wrap a bouncy football,
Or a unicorn that rocks...

I can battle with the sticky tape.
Or snip a sheet just SO!
I can write a fancy label,
I can tie a shiny bow.

I am all stuck-up with glitter,
I've been wrapping night and day -
I sometimes think I might have gone
And wrapped my life away...

I'm your perfect Present-Wrapper,
(Though I know I shouldn't boast)
But don't look out for gifts from me -
Your Cash is in the post!

THE CHRISTMAS BAZAAR.
****

(Spoken by a Vicar - whose new teeth don't quite fit...)

Oh! Do come along to our Christmas Bazaar -
The entrance is over there.
It's all run by dear Mrs. Buggins - She's the one with astonishing hair;
And she's manning our Crafty-Craft Stall
With her usual, festive flair.

Her circle of well-managed ladies
Make ALL of the goodies themselves.
Snowmen they stuff with old dish cloths - To brighten your dining-room shelves.
Ingenious hand-knitted items,
Like jolly green camels. And elves...

And hats in a HUGE range of sizes,
Recycled from cast-away socks.
Or else, a Nativity collage - Assembled from bits of old clocks!
Or jam-jars to swing from the ceiling,
Or snowflakes, hand-painted on rocks.

There's a Santa-Claus stitched from old jumpers,
Who seems to turn up every year -
His eyes are a tiny bit creepy - So he can cause a smidgen of fear,
But he's ALWAYS first prize in the Raffle
So DO buy a ticket, my dear.

And then there's our merry Tombola,
With treasures from last Christmas Day -
Plenty of soaps. And strange objects - That kind-
hearted folk give away.
You've drawn out a FIVE! Aren't you lucky?
You've just won a Nit-Killer Spray.

Just look at our table of Produce...
The cakes are a total delight,
The icing is JOYFULLY vibrant - It was spread by the
Toddlers last night.
And I'm sure it will set by next Friday...
My dear - are you feeling all right?

You ARE looking awfuly queasy -
What you need is medicinal Honey.
The bees come from Mr. Finn's Fish-Farm - So
sometimes it smells a bit funny,
But...Oh! The poor fellow's escaping -
Thank goodness we took all his money!

****

THE CHOICE.
****

Charities know how to get at my money -
A tray full of toys, labelled 'Festive and Funny'.

I sort out my coins and I honestly try
To make my selection. I hover. I sigh...

The poor little Penguin? The brave little Bear?
I study them all, since I want to be fair.

The sorrowful Snowman? The droopy-eyed Deer?
I've stood here for ages. It feels like a year.

The wobbly Robin. Which one shall I choose?
I'm meant to be buying some cough sweets. And shoes...

The Fairy's forlorn, and the Gnome breaks my heart.
I pick one. Replace it. I'm falling apart.

They ALL seem to need me. What choice have I got?
At last...I've decided!
I've bought the whole lot.

****

THE CHRISTMAS RAFFLE.

Oh no! It's the Raffle! It has to be done -
I know that it's meant to be innocent fun;
I know that I COULD be the fortunate one.

A fabulous hamper of food could be mine;
A bouquet of roses; a cruise down the Rhine;
A huge box of biscuits, a bottle of wine.

A cuddly Penguin; a spoon carved from wood -
And all for a cause that's incredibly good...
So I ought to be keen - but I'd hide if I could.

The girl stands beside me, her smile fixed like glue.
She offers a pink slip, she offers a blue.
I only want one - but I'll have to buy two.

And now comes the moment I loathe and I dread...
Out come the tickets. A yellow? A red?
And BOTH of them claimed by a stranger called Ned.

Out come more numbers. Too high and too low.
So near, yet so far. Just a few gifts to go...
I'm ALWAYS unlucky. My gloom starts to grow.

The torture continues. I cover my eyes.
The last number's called - and I shriek with surprise.
I've finally cracked it! I've landed a prize.

An unwanted object is left on the shelf,
A horrible, hideous, pointy-eared Elf...
And I'm handed the thing
I donated MYSELF.

****

THE THIEF IN THE SHOP.

(This poem is based on a true story.)

The Thief in the Shop
Saw the gifts round the tree;
Glittery parcels, donated for free -
And intended for children with little. Or less.
Whose parents were poor, and whose lives were a mess.

The Thief in the Shop
With a cynical sneer
Grabbed a great handful. Why not? They were here.
Unguarded, uncounted and paid for by fools.
The Camera watched him reject Christmas rules.

The Thief in the Shop
Soon appeared on T.V.
His face was too hooded and hazy to see.
He couldn't be captured or given a name -
But he saw his own actions...and shuddered with shame.

The Thief in the Shop
In his hood (as before)
Returned all toys - plus a whole sackful more!
The Camera watched with a wise, patient eye -
As a kindlier man waved a grateful:
'Good Bye.'

BREADLINE BLUES.
****

I'm out of work this Christmas.
I'm in a proper mess -
My children both need lap-tops,
My wife would love a dress.

But no one wants my knowledge,
My labour or my skills -
So how can I buy presents?
I can't pay half the bills.

The kids don't want a promise -
They want a proper tree,
And though my wife won't say it,
I'm sure they're blaming me.

My love won't grant their wishes -
And kisses won't buy toys...
They won't be finding presents
Like the other girls and boys.

And how can I explain it,
Or face them with the truth?
What kind of father am I
To rob them of their youth?

The Christmas Lists they've written
Are waiting on the shelf,
But no one comes to read them -
Except perhaps myself.

'Dear Santa,
We're writing to tell you
To take our new lap-tops right back.
We only want Dad to be happy -
So just bring a JOB in your sack.'

X X X

A MERRY RECESSION.
****

The Credit Crunch can get us down -
We read our statements with a frown;
We fret about the Christmas treats -
The children's toys, the food, the sweets.

But do we want a huge expence
To strain our nerves and steal our pence?
Or would we rather smile, relax.
Forget about the Income Tax...

And just make do with cheaper things -
Home-made gifts and stars on strings.
Silly games with foolish prizes,
Hugs and smiles and daft surprises.

Have an indoor snowball fight
With cotton wool - it's soft and white!
Dance around a twiggy tree,
Swap old jokes at Christmas tea.

Fill the air with kindly words;
Share our breadcrumbs with the birds.
Take a walk and wave at friends,
Fool around till daylight ends.

Then hold hands and dim the lights,
Tell a tale of spooks and sprites!
Feel the cheery Christmas glow
That used to warm us, long ago...

Recessions can be tough, it's true,
For worriers, like me. And you.
But sometimes they can make us see
Our love and laughter come for
FREE.

****

THE HAMPER.
****

The room was damp, the migrants cold.
Their hopes were gone. Their treasures sold -
Then someone, softly tapped the door...
The mother froze.
The father swore -

Another vandal, keen to sneer -
Or kick them out, now storms grew near.
He turned the key, prepared to fight...
A hamper stood
In pools of light.

But who had found their sad address?
The silver tag said: 'Happiness'.
A cruel joke to tease the poor?
He raised the lid,
A crack. No more...

Then Joy spilled out across the floor.

The children gazed at festive treats,
The tiny toys. The Christmas sweets.
The woolly scarves, as soft as fur,
And socks. And gloves -
For him. For her.

The mother almost wept to see
The home-made cakes, the tinsel tree,
The scarlet crackers full of fun,
And loaves as warm
As summer sun.

The old ones smiled. They rubbed their eyes.

Brand new boots - the perfect size.
While father found a cap to wear -
A fleecy jacket,
Packed with care.

And no one knew who came that night,
To lift the darkness. Put things right.
Perhaps a Saint in scarlet hood?
Or simply someone kind. And good,
Who crept away
As angels should.

****

HAPPINESS HAMPERS DOT COM...
****

One year, I discovered a Website - Which offered us Christmas Day Fun:
'Happiness Hampers - The Present That Pampers'
With something for EVERY ONE.
So I typed out a list on my laptop -
I almost exhausted my wits...
With choices and sizes - for tasty surprises
To thrill the whole family to bits.

The Hamper appeared on our doorstep - It was wide, it was weighty...and whiffy,
So we heaved it inside - with excitement and pride
And snipped through the strings in a jiffy!
The lid gave a creak and flew open
As bubble-wrap burst on the floor,
Then we dug through the layers - like Treasure-Hunt players
To excavate goodies galore.

There were jars full of glittery syrup - from Treacle Mines fragrant and deep.
There was Icelandic Cheese - made from milk you can squeeze
From a Walrus (make sure she's asleep)!
There were combs full of extra-dark Honey
Which glued our old Gran to her chair.
There were 'Pickles in Pots' - which gave us pink spots...
While the 'Dynamite Sauce' frizzed our hair.

There were bottles of wine from an Island -
Consisting of Volcanic Rocks.
The aroma was teasing - it left us all sneezing...
The taste was like yesterday's socks.
There were bowls full of stuff from a forest - That bubbled and quietly floated...
So our nerves were in shreds - when we spotted the heads
OF INSECTS!
All chocolate coated...

Then we noticed a box wrapped in ribbons - Which looked like a gift from a Queen.
So we thought we would risk it - and nibbled a biscuit...
But even the Poodle turned green!
And yet...
The whole thing was a triumph!
We were Gourmets. The Stars of the Street!
All the neighbours came round - with a buzz and a bound,
There was laughter and plenty to eat...

SO

Our Christmas was voted a Winner!
A feast without tension or stress...
And our Hamper's still stacked - With the friendships we packed,
Plus
The secret of true
HAPPINESS.

****

CHRISTMAS COMPANY

REINDEER RAP.
****

We're a groovy team,
We're a hot-hoof band,
With our jingle bells
From a magic land.
When we pull that sleigh,
When we go, man, go,
When we bring F.C.
With his Ho! Ho! Ho!
When we get on down
To your sleepy street;
When we rock your roof
To a hip-hop beat;
When we stomp away
Through the starry sky;
You can make a wish
As we boogy-by.
You can shake your hands,
You can stamp your toe,
You can strut your stuff
In the cool, Yule snow.
You can shout and cheer,
Set the whole world clapping -
We're the Reindeer Band
And we're Christmas Rapping!

****

'TIS THE SEASON FOR A SELFIE.
****

(Spoken by Santa!)

"Oh look! Rudolph's sent me a Selfie.
There he is, peeping over his door.
He wants me to say that: 'I Like Him' -
Though I've told him quite often before..."

"In fact, he's sent DOZENS of Selfie's
To the Gnomes and the Penguins and Me -
Rudolph in front of the Grotto;
Rudolph on top of the Tree;
Rudolph with Frosty the Snowman;
Or munching a massive mince-pie;
Or dressed in the Fairy's pink tu-tu...
Or zooming around in the sky."

"Rudolph in HUNDREDS of poses;
Yet still he keeps sending me more!
Rudolph in so many places,
He's quickly becoming a bore.
Good grief! He's just sent me another
Though it's late and I'm tucked up in bed -
Rudolph dressed up as a Robot
With an aerial stuck on his head."

"I've seen him with Soap Stars and Heroes,
At Someone's Celebrity Ball -
Sometimes I catch myself hoping
He'll slip on a carrot and fall!
I've tried to be terribly patient,
But when will this Selfie Stuff end?
If he pulls any more funny faces
I'll finally go round the bend."

"OH NO!
Here's a photo of Rudolph -
In tights!" Santa says with a groan.
"If he sends any more - I'll be SELFISH
And I'll just have to STAMP
On his phone!"

****

RUDOLPH'S BACK.
****
(This year, things are worse!)

Rudolph loves his i-Pod, so
He's constantly Dot-Comming;
And now he's tested all his Apps -
He's into Photo-Bombing!

He's THERE, beside the Fairy
At the top of Santa's tree-
Which means the Safety Elf has found
Pine-needles in his tea!
And look! A set of antlers
Behind the Gnomes - how rude.
So Rudolph's wrecked their Group-Hug
And he's spoiled their festive mood.

Now Mrs. Santa's fuming -
Each photograph this year
Includes a blurry nose-bag, or
A hoof or two. Oh Deer!
And Mr. Snowman's selfie - well!
That jolly moment's lost...HE
Clicked as Rudolph chewed his hat
So now he's REALLY Frosty.

And even Percy Penguin
Smartly dressed to take a paddle,
Was sad to see his bathing suit
Obscured by Rudolph's saddle.
BUT
Wise old Santa's hatched a plan -
This year, on Christmas night,
When Rudolph poses on the roof
With nose all shiny bright...

His friends will PHOTO-BOMB him,
And they'll yell:
"IT SERVES YOU RIGHT."

****

WHAT SHALL WE DO WITH THE RED-NOSED REINDEER.
****

Verse One:
What shall we do with the Red-Nosed Reindeer?
What shall we do with the Red-Nosed Reindeer?
What shall we do with the Red-Nosed Reindeer
On our Christmas Morning.

Verse Two:
Pop him in a stocking to surprise Aunt Mary,
Fix him on a fir-tree with the Christmas Fairy,
Let him pull a milk-float to the local Dairy,
On our Christmas Morning.

Chorus:
Hooray! We like surprises. Hooray! We like surprises.
Hooray! We like surprises - On our Christmas
Morning.

Verse One Again...

Verse Three:
Make him feel embarrassed in a silly sweater,
Take him to the Pantomime until he's better,
Send him back to Santa with a 'Thank You' letter,
On our Christmas Morning.

Verse One Again - Repeat Chorus...

Verse Four:
That's what we'll do with the Red-Nosed Reindeer,
Tell him that we're hoping that he'll come back soon dear...
Wonder if he's sorry that he EVER came here,
On our Christmas Morning.

****

THE CHRISTMAS CONTEST.
****

In the Grotto, excitement was mounting - The
Contest was nearing its close,
As eight hopeful Reindeer were waiting
To see who had won - by a nose!
The Judges were Santa and Rudolph - A Penguin, a
Bear and a Gnome...
While two jolly Snowmen with joke-books
Were making the crowd feel at home.

The first nervous singer was Prancer - Whose throat
was all croaky and dry -
Then Dancer sang loudly (but badly)
And ran off to have a good cry!
Dasher was dressed in an outfit - Designed to
astound and delight...
(A pity the leather kept creaking -
And the saddle was clearly too tight).

Vixen was sexy and sultry - So nobody cared how
she sang!
Then Cupid came on as a Cracker!
So HER number went with a BANG.
Comet was quick, but quite sparky - Donner was cool
and controlled;
Blitzen was simply AMAZING...
Until she gave Santa her cold.

The tension grew tighter and tighter - The Snowmen grew sweaty and small...
The Judges consulted and argued
Then dished out their comments to all...
Santa was kind (as expected) - And said they were ALL very nice.
The Penguin just giggled and nodded,
The Gnome offered helpful advice.

But Rudolph (quite frankly) was callous - He criticised, snorted and sneered -
So the Bear bashed his shiny, red hooter...
While the audience stood up and cheered!
Just then - they heard tinkly music - As the Fairy flapped down from her tree -
She said: "The whole team should have contracts."
And EVERYONE yelled: "We agree!"

So the Reindeer zoomed-off to sing carols
Together! On Christmas T.V.
While Rudolph clopped home to his stable
And ate 'Humble Pie' for his tea!

****

THE POLAR BEAR POEM.
****

"I'm not a greedy creature,
Said the gloomy Polar Bear -
"I don't want fancy fittings for my private, winter lair.
I don't want fancy clothing,
Since I'm rather fond of fur.
I don't want fancy dinners - frozen food's what I prefer."

"I'm not a fat and friendly bear
Who wants a pot of honey.
And I don't do any shopping - so I don't want any
money -
I don't want fancy footwear
Since my paws are made of leather;
I don't want tubes of sun-cream - since I
don't have sunny weather."

"I don't want fluffy duvets
Or a cosy, rocking chair,
So - I'm not a greedy creature - sighed
the gloomy, Polar Bear.
BUT!
Life is rather boring
In a land of ice and snow,
So I would be REALLY grateful - If your Sleigh could
swoop quite low -
Then whizz me round the midnight sky...
With Rudolph:
"OFF WE GO!"

****

(And let's hope his icy world will still be here for
ever...?)

DRONING ON.
****

(Spoken by Father Christmas.)

This Winter,
I went and swapped Rudolph
For a gadget that flies on its own!
Not a milk-float or lorry,
Or posh Waitrose trolley -
But a High-Speed Delivery Drone!

Which means that you won't hear (at midnight)
A jingle or clattering hoof,
Since the point of a Drone
Is - it drops like a stone
And demolishes most of your roof.

So don't ask for anything fragile,
Or presents that weigh half a ton -
If they land on your head
And they flatten your bed,
Your Christmas won't feature much fun.

Of course, you could all write a letter
And ask me to dig out the sleigh -
It's creaky and tragic...
But powered by MAGIC
And that's what you love.
CHOCKS AWAY!

****

THE ELF AND SAFETY RAP.
****

We're a mean, green team -
We're the Safety Elves,
We will take the tinsel from your Toy Shop shelves...

We will grab your guns
(Which is no surprise);
We will ban the bears with their beady eyes.
We will scrap the kits
With the tiny parts;
We will seize the box with the plastic darts.

We will pulp your paints
(They can make you sick)
We will crush the cars that you just might lick.
We will swipe the swings
And the slippy slide;
We will slice the dolly with the spikes inside!

We will snatch the scooters
That you want to buy;
We will shake our heads when you start to cry.
We will Read the Rules,
We will wreck your day -
Then we'll smash your gadgets - and we'll stamp away.

We're the Safety Elves,
And our work's begun -
We're a mean, green team - and we're having FUN!

****

E. L. F.
****

(On behalf Of - The Elf Liberation Front.)

Every year we grumble at the endless, midnight hours;
Let alone the Workshop noise - the toppled Lego Towers;
Frost-bite on our ears and toes. No rest. No rights. No powers.

Elves are always overlooked - and just because we're small,
Life should not be one long drag, ignored by one and all...
Fighting for a scrap of space, to wrap a bat and ball.

Even Christmas Fairies win a starring role for free!
Looking cute and rather smug on Santa's shiny tree...
Forgetting all the the frozen folk, still packing - frenziedly.

Each gift, whatever size or shape (I'll mention Unicorns,
Large and lumpy Teddy Bears, or Bikes with bells and horns) -
Fall to Elves with paper-cuts and scissors sharp as thorns!

Elvish Representatives should call a strike and say:
"Learn your Elf & Safety Code. Right now, without delay!
Find your Wrapping Rules and SUE - the Grotto Gnomes today."

"End this Yuletide torment NOW. Speak out ! Be proud ! Be Green.
Let Old Father Christmas know you're moody, mad and mean !
Fill your Festive Banner with a slogan bold and blunt."

        'Elves Unite! And join us in our
        Liberation
        Front.'

****

THE IGLOO BLUES.
****
(For a very tall Elf!)

"I'm a HUGE hungry Elf, and my chocolate money
Was spent on my rent, so my life isn't funny.
I'm out in the cold
Which is not very nice
My nose has gone red and it's dripping with ice."

"I've stayed by the Grotto for long, frosty ages,
Wishing for work and a big bag of wages..
I wish I could welcome
A Christmassy Queue,
And choose jolly presents for people like you."

"I'd always be cheerful and warm by the fire,
With the Penguins, the Fairy,
The Snow-Ladies Choir.
But instead I just shiver and try not to sniff -
Though my raggy, green jumper
Is frozen and stiff!"

"Now my toes have gone numb, in my old, pointy shoes -
So here I am - singing
My sad, Winter Blues:
A GIANT-SIZED ELF isn't wanted today...
But wait! I've been hired
To help Santa! Hooray!"

"He's paid me a FORTUNE - To push-start his Sleigh."

****

SANTA'S SOLILOQUY.
****

(Or: 'Grotto Grumble' - For Ted.)

This isn't the part I'd choose you know -
I wanted to be MacDuff,
Strutting the stage in a tartan kilt
And spouting that Scottish stuff.

I wanted to be Renaissance Man,
A Hamlet of tragic power:
I wanted to wear a Donkey's head
And snooze in a magic bower.
I wanted to be an evil King
With a hump and a squeaky voice!
I wanted to be Mark Antony -
The moody Egyptian's choice.

I wanted to be a bluff King Hal
Who married six merry wives;
I wanted to dare the Ides of March
Betrayed by old friends with knives.
I wanted to be Lord Prospero
And rule an enchanted land;
I wanted to be a Warrior
With blood dripping from each hand.

I wanted to be young Romeo
Who wept in a ghostly tomb;
I wanted to be the jealous Moor
To seal Desdemona's doom.
I wanted to stun the R.S.C.
With scenes from my great King Lear;
I wanted to be the Grand Old Man
And win an award each year.

But Actors are bound to be typecast -
"The part is so YOU," they explain...
So that's why I'm stuck in this Grotto
And dressed up as Santa
AGAIN!

****

A CLOSE SHAVE.
****

It was Christmas Day in the Workshop
And Santa was resting at home -
In excitement he opened a parcel
To discover - a spray-can of foam.
'You too could be smooth as a Snowman'
It announced, as he ruffled his jaw.
With a frown he examined the label -
A gift from his Mother-in-Law!

This was something he often had dreaded,
A moment he often had feared...
She could cope with the boots and the reindeer,
But she couldn't put up with his beard!
"It's all very well for your Mother,"
He complained as his Wife pottered in...
"But how can I fly round at midnight
In the cold - with no fluff on my chin?"

"I'll be frozen and covered in chilblains,
I'll be shivering all Christmas Eve,
I'll have sneezing fits over stockings -
And then what will children believe?
Let's face it - it just isn't Christmas
If Santa's not properly dressed
In a bright, rosy hat with a bobble
And a pile of white curls down my chest?"

At that moment - the door thundered open,
As Mother strode firmly inside -
(She was known by the gnomes and the penguins
As 'She Who Must Not Be Defied').
"Come on Santa," she roared like a Fog-Horn,
(An icicle fell off the wall)
"Here's a razor - now, off to the bathroom."
There was no chance to argue at all!

With a shudder, he stood by the mirror
And waved his reflection good-bye!
Then sadly attacked his moustaches
While trying his best not to cry.
So now
If you go to see Santa
He still has his merry old looks...
But his beard seems a tiny bit wobbly -
And you'll notice
It's held up with hooks!

In fact, you may even be thinking,
The whole thing is cheap, cotton-wool:
But please don't upset Santa's feelings
By giving his whiskers a pull...
Remember -
He USED to be handsome
With a beard like a Polar-Bear Rug!
So pretend that you just haven't noticed,
And give him a big
Christmas hug.

****

'TIS THE SEASON TO BE HAIRY.
****

(For Martin.)

Beards are BACK!
They're trending -
Are they laughed at?
No -
They're NOT...

The change has taken ages, but
At last they've hit the spot.
So hairy men are happy -
No more shaving cuts
To blot.

The Ogre now can strut his stuff,
Prince Charming's lost
The plot!
The Werewolf's feeling really smug -
With all the hair
He's got.

And Sportsmen have decided
To give the thing
A shot -
They can choose a saucy Goatee,
Or a Wizard's
Tangled knot...

While T.V. Stars have all begun
To sprout a
Splendid lot
Of facial decorations like
King Kong
Or Captain Scott.

Which means: this year
Old Santa's COOL...
Or very, very
HOT!

****

THE SANTA SCHOOL RAP.
****

(Don't let your small children hear this one!)

In a Far-Off Land - By a frozen pool,
There's a sign to say - 'This Is Santa-School'.

You can spot a crowd
Full of cheerful chaps,
Who have mince-pie crumbs on their knees and laps.
They are all dressed up in their Uniforms,
There are woolly vests
For the winter storms.
There are big, white beards which are fixed on hooks,
(Like the ones you see
In your picture books).
There are scarlet coats; there are boots and hoods;
There are bulgy tummies
Full of Christmas Puds!

When the lessons start
Mister Merry tells
How to start a sleigh. How to jingle bells.
How to steer the Deer round a block of flats,
Or a Satellite
Or a swoop of bats.
They must learn to cope with a HUGE G-FORCE;
When the Reindeer race
Past a rocket. Or horse.
They must stuff a sock - with the gifts and toys,
They must creep round rooms
Making NOT ONE noise.

But the biggest test
And the worst of all
(When December comes and the snowflakes fall)

When the Grotto Queue grows a bit too long,
And the Snowmen moan
At the same old song...

Then the children whine - So the grown-ups glare,
And the Fairies groan
As they tear their hair...
That is JUST the time - when the Santa's know
They must greet each child
With a: "Ho! Ho! HO!"

Then their Teacher,
Who
Is a kindly bloke,
Will conclude their course
With His Christmas Joke:

"You have ALL done well -
You have stayed on track,
SO
I simply must - give you all...

THE SACK!"

****

SANTA'S SPOOKY CHRISTMAS.
****

There's a story they tell in the Igloo
When Winter's beginning to bite
Of the time when Old Santa was given
A rather unseasonal fright.
The whole thing began with a letter
(The writing was scrawly and red)
'Please bring a few gifts to my Castle -
And DON'T wait till sunrise,' it said.

'Bring goblets all smothered in jewels,
And bandages, brand new and white -
A toothbrush (much larger than normal)
Some candles that drip when alight.
Some juicy, fresh flies for the spiders,
Some bones for the great, castle hound -
And one or two night-scented flowers
To perfume the air - underground.'

So Santa prepared the surprises
And bundled them all in the sleigh...
(His wife packed his flask and his lunchbox,
Then waved as he sped on his way).
He soared through the air like a shadow,
That cast its dark shape on the Moon -
He raced round the dark like a demon
Then stirred his cold tea with a spoon.

The sandwiches seemed to taste funny
But he wasn't the sort to complain -
So he swallowed the very last morsel
And searched for the castle again!
Below him the towers loomed skywards,
The place looked deserted and wild...
As Santa touched down on a turret
Where gargoyles all greedily smiled!

He soon found his way to a bedroom
With curtains of torn, scarlet lace -
There were cobwebs hung over the stockings
As bats flapped their wings in his face.
Then Someone rose up beside Santa -
A figure incredibly tall!
His cape was as magic as midnight
(His mirror was blank on the wall).

Those eyes glowed like dangerous embers;
His icicle fangs drooled with lust -
Then Santa was shoved up the chimney
While Somebody howled: "All Is Dust!"
Now, Santa clumped back to the reindeer,
They snorted and started to sniff.
But the poor chap was covered in goose-bumps
So nobody mentioned the whiff!

****

Next night, snuggled warm in his jim-jams
He dreamed of that terrible room -
The monster, the teeth and the mirror...
The sickening feeling of doom!
But his wife softly snored on her pillow,
Untroubled by mid-winter chills,
Knowing a nice GARLIC sandwich
Had kept Santa safe from
ALL CHILLS!

****

JUST A NOTE AT TWILIGHT.
****

(To be spoken - or sung to the tune of: 'Twinkle, Twinkle, Little Star'.)

Santa,
I would like to get,
Just for me - a Vampire pet.
Must be handsome. Must be tall,
Must be keen to climb my wall.
Must have eyes that glow and stare,
Must have velvet cloaks to wear.

Should have super flying skills,
Moonlit dives for midnight thrills.
Also, fangs that shine like ice -
Biting's banned. It isn't nice.

If this breaches protocol -
Send a Werewolf...

Kiss, Kiss,

L.O.L.

****

IF YOU GO DOWN TO THE MALL TODAY...
****

The Merry Mall was shining - All the decorations dangled.
The tree-top fairy twinkled and the silver sleighbells jangled.
The shops were crammed and crowded, since the outdoor world was chilly -
But Mister Squeak, who blew balloons, was seasonally silly!

The toys were truly tempting and the fashions really ritzy...
The jolly Christmas Grotto by the cash-machine was glitzy!
But no one seemed to notice that the mood was turning gloomy;
That all the lifts were creaky and the snowman songs were doomy.

So no one spied the tell-tale trails of bandages and blood.
No one heard a shuffle or a sudden, muffled thud...
But the ghastly groans grew louder and the mournful moans grew creepy.
Mothers whimpered, children wailed - and tattooed Dads felt weepy.

They tried to run, they tried to find an Exit to the town,
But all the doors were bolted as the dark came swooping down,
The Phantoms and the Zombies, they were lurching left and right,
Their stuck-out arms set off alarms - while Bouncers fled in fright.

And THEN a swarm of Vampires flapped around with pointy teeth,
Which wasn't fun for anyone who wandered underneath!
The screaming staff and customers - their legs had turned to jelly,
This wasn't like the horror films they laughed at on the telly!

They formed a frenzied huddle, where they shivered and they shook -
The snarling Spooks prepared to pounce - but no one dared to look!
And just as everybody thought their final moment loomed...
A massive Scarlet Shape rose up - and 'HO! Ho! Ho!' it boomed.

In seconds, all the Monsters lost the plot and skipped away -
With lots of lovely presents and with happy smiles! Hooray!
But WHO defeated all the Fiends? A Werewolf? Who could say?
Or was it Santa Claws - Who flashed his Fangs And saved the day!

****

MOTHER CHRISTMAS.
****

We all know that Santa is magic
(Which is how he gets into our homes).
We all know he fills up the stockings
With toys made by toy-making Gnomes.

We know that he keeps teams of reindeer,
And rides round the World in his sleigh...
We know that he wears a red jacket
And lives in a land far away.

But what about old Mother Christmas?
We don't know a thing about her!
Like, does she wear big, scarlet knickers
And does she make mince pies all year?

And are her cheeks rosy as berries?
And are her eyes sparky and bright?
And does she like wrapping the presents?
And does she sing carols all night?

And does she goes shopping for carrots
And treats for the Christmas Eve crew?
Does she read ALL the long letters
From grown ups like me and like you?

And does she knit hats for the Snowmen?
And does she hang cards on the door?
And does she make Santa wear slippers,
When sooty old boots smudge the floor?

And does she like dancing with Penguins?
And does she love crackers? And snow?
And does she make EVERYONE happy?

I bet that your Mother will know!

****

A MERRY MUDDLE.
****

Old Santa chose new glasses - the complicated sort
That sadly weren't as magical and manly as he thought.

For one thing, they were wonky - For another, they were blurred,
So when the Christmas postbag came
He couldn't read a word.
He squinted through his lenses, he tried his level best,
But in the gloom of Winter, well...
He panicked. Then he guessed!

That's why, on Christmas morning, our Gran was given flippers,
Although this year she clearly asked
For comfy tartan slippers.
While darling little Daisy found a python by the tree...
She scares the neighbours half to death
Although she's only three.

And Bob, who rides a motorbike has frilly frocks to wear,
So just for once, we think he's right
To mutter: "It's not fair."
As for Mum - she's moaning. She wanted something smart -
But not a weird picture of
A gloomy work of art.

Only Dad was cheerful - although we can't think why.
Perhaps a plastic pirate ship
Is better than a tie?
Perhaps YOU'VE had disasters too - perhaps YOUR heart has sunk?
When groping through your stocking
You've discovered heaps of junk!

Perhaps Old Santa should be told - by phone, or text or letter:
Don't buy glasses from the Gnomes...
Opticians would be better!

****

TALES BY TORCH-LIGHT

A WINTER'S TALE.
****

Draw the curtains,
Dim the lights -
Tell us a tale for frosty nights.

Hear how the breeze in the twisted trees
Mourns for each fallen leaf.
See how the rain on the shining pane
Weeps for a private grief...
And learn how a child on an evening wild
Was branded a shameless thief.

Just as the snow touched the earth below
Cold as the kiss of Fate,
A pitiful cry shook the frozen sky,
Wailed at the Workhouse Gate.
An innocent heart, too soon would depart
And pity would come too late.

At dawn of day, as the stars fled away,
Truth was a glinting knife;
Bright as the frost shone a bracelet lost -
Dropped by a careless wife.
And clasped once again, hung the golden chain -
The price of a stolen life.

Hear how the breeze in the twisted trees
Sobs like a soul in fear;
See how the rain on the shining pane
Weeps with a salty tear.
And grieve for the child - eyes hollow and wild,
Who watches our feast each year...

Draw the curtains,
Dim the lights,
Tell us a tale for frosty nights.

****

THE GHOST HORSES.

1914 - 1918.

Well, we all stood and waved as they clattered away:
Black Bess and old Dob and our daft Dapple Grey.

But young Percy - he wept,
So we soothed him with lies...
They'd have fine wooden stables. They'd see bright,
foreign skies.
They'd never know hunger,
Nor hardship, nor cold -
But fields full of clover and horseshoes of gold.

Their days would be lazy,
Their saddles would gleam.
They would eat from a manger and drink from a stream
So clear and so sweet -
They'd be youthful once more,
And they'd never hear guns, or a whisper of war.

But the years trotted by
And young Percy grew wise:
Too sick of the truth and his poor mother's cries,
To listen to stories -
But one winter's night
When the Moon lined our yard with a pathway of light...

We all heard the hoofbeats,
We all saw again
The flick of a tail and the shake of a mane -
And there, in the meadow
(I swear this is true)
Three horses were rolling in clover. And dew.

Well, we all stood and wept as they faded away -
Black Bess and Old Dob and our daft Dapple Grey.

CHRISTMAS AT HOME.
****
1916.

He staggered back in the dug-out
Soaked by the merciless rain,
But his heart was home in England
Far from the the drum-beat of pain.

The trenches echoed with gunfire,
A cry from the edge of Hell,
But all he heard was a songbird
And the chime of a Christmas bell.

He drifted through the shadows
Of a world he had left behind:
Till hate and fear and poison gas
Were blotted from his mind.

He climbed a misty pathway,
He walked a frosty street,
He caught the scent of lavender
That bathed his weary feet.

He stepped inside a hallway,
He cast his rifle down,
He breathed the sleepy warmth of her,
The softness of her gown.

The room was trimmed with holly,
A wreath hung by the door -
Blood-red berries, leaves so sharp
They seemed to speak of war.

He kissed her twining fingers,
He stroked her drooping hair -
He gently, gently crept away
As morning shook the air.

And searching in the dawnlight,
They found him where he slept -
Stiff and cold in the dug-out
While foreign rainclouds wept...

But she sat by the ashes
Of a fire that once burned bright -
And knew her man had come to her
For one last Christmas night.

****

THE STRANGER'S STORY.
****

The hour was late when the Stranger
came to the moor's bleak edge.
The short cut - was dangerous but
he was lured from the guiding hedge.

All for the gift he carried
and the message he must bear.
He paid heed - to his greater need,
though his conscience might cry: "Beware!"

The wind grew icy and savage
gnawing his flesh like teeth -
Black as pitch - gaped a waiting ditch
As it snatched a prey for the heath...

Out of the murderous darkness
in a weaving mesh of fog,
Lifting jowls - with curdling howls
rose the massive form of a dog.

It flung itself at the Stranger -
And its coat was thick and warm.
So it lay - till the streaks of day
brought a rescuer with the dawn.

****

The Stranger leaned on the pillows
and spoke from his drowsy bed -
"Was he yours? That dog on the moors...
but for him, I was surely dead."

"Ah, no," said the man. "My Pilot,
he died, ten years ago.
Tired an old - and stiffened with cold
from saving a man
in the snow."

****

FOOTPRINTS IN THE SNOW.

The sunlit hillsides beckoned me,
A frosty summit shone,
But pathways strayed - from brook and glade
Till hope and sense had gone.

The daylight faded swiftly,
A darkness swooped like Death.
My flesh grew cold - as fear took hold,
I climbed with rasping breath...
While hungry winds prowled round me
With growls so crazed and wild
I slid on stones -as sharp as bones.
I whimpered like a child.

Then snow, in suffocating waves
Erased each rock and track,
The blizzard screamed - yet something seemed
To call me - call me back.
I stumbled from my shallow grave,
Saw footprints in the snow.
I followed where - the dents lay bare,
My steps were pained and slow.

The trail became a labyrinth,
It coiled towards a tower
And as I stared - a candle flared
To light that haunted hour.
I pushed the wormy door with dread
To face what lurked inside...
An iron bed - a hunk of bread,
No sign of ghost. Or guide.

The dusty window shuddered
While the air grew soft and kind.
Too weak for pride - I stood and cried:
"They'll say I've lost my mind.
And yet, my unseen friend, you came
To find me where I lay,
You snapped the snare - of my despair
You marked a wiser way."

Long years have turned. My stories drift,
But still, one truth I know:
When demons raved - my life was saved
By footprints in the snow..

****

THE CRY.
****

As I hurried through the city - I heard a child's thin cry -
"For pity's sake, please help me,"
But the shoppers scurried by.
And no one stopped to listen,
No one saw the boy.
His voice was drowned by music - It sang of hope and joy.

I glanced at shining windows - I raced from store to store,
"For pity's sake, please help me,"
I heard the cry once more.
But my mind was was full of Christmas
The presents I must buy,
I had no time for strangers - No time for where or why.

I struggled past an alley - The words were frail and near,
"For pity's sake, please help me."
I felt the grip of fear.
I gathered up my parcels,
I clutched them safe and tight;
I turned away from shadows - I fled towards the light.

Yet always, in the darkness - I hear the child's thin cry:
"For pity's sake, please help me."
Too late I stop and sigh.
I search the haunted doorways
For an echo of his name -
But the child is lost forever - And my soul cries out in shame.

****

THE PHANTOM RIDER.
****

I was weary and homesick and hungry - When I came to a lonely Inn;
I tied my horse to the gatepost
As the moonlight grew watery-thin.
And I did not look at the Rider - Who followed my path like a twin.

Chorus: The Phantom Rider - All cloaked and grey,
He'll follow you all - One day, one day...

I huddled beside a bare window - Thick with a curtain of grime,
And I scooped my soup like an orphan
Lost in a long-ago rhyme..
While Somebody deep in the darkness - Was scooping and scraping in time.
I flung my coins in a hurry - I was eager to canter away.
My horse was in need of a stable
His bed in the sweet-smelling hay;
And I would be glad of a welcome - The warmth and the safety of day.

(Chorus)

But behind me, I heard a faint rhythm - Of hoofs on the hazardous track;
A rattle, like bones in a graveyard,
So clear - yet I dared not look back,
For fear of the Phantom who followed - Who hunted like hounds in a pack.
The thud of the hoof-beats grew louder - They chilled me far more than the hail.
Was there no one to rise up and save me'

From the fiend who was haunting my trail?
It was then that my horse slipped and tumbled - And I fell with a pitiful wail.

(Chorus)

I sprawled in the mud and I whimpered - he loomed like a Demon. Or worse.
His voice was as cold as an iceberg -
It frosted my flesh like a curse...
As he stretched out his skeleton fingers - And he groaned like the creak of a hearse:

(Chorus)

"When you fled like a fool from a nightmare -
Something fell at my feet...
"HERE'S YOUR PURSE!"

****

THE ROLLRIGHT STONES.

Beneath the stars a circle stands,
Carved and curved by unknown hands,
Set on high by mighty men -
But who can tell me why, or when?
My questions whirl and drift away...
The stones keep silence and will not say.

Did a leader, strong and wise
Raise this tribute to the skies?
Or did a witch with crafty spell
Charm a King (as people tell)
And turn his soldiers cold and grey?
The stones keep silence and will not say.

Here's the hushed and scattered crowd,
Here's the King Stone, tall and proud;
Here, below the misty lights,
Still as death, the Whispering Knights.
Do they grieve, or dream, or pray?
The stones keep silence and will not say.

Is it true, when midnight passes,
The captives stir amongst the grasses
And softly creep towards a spring
To quench the thirst of knight and King?
And do they dread the dawn's first ray?
The stones keep silence and will not say.

Mystic shrine or ancient tomb?
Your legends lurk where shadows loom,
Your secrets hide like buried gold,
Your truth is deep and dark and old.
My questions whirl and drift away...
The stones keep silence - and will not say.

****

(The legend says that a King and his men were
turned to stone by a wily witch -
who cried: "Stick, stock, stone!" And they stand there
still...)

THE CHIME CHILD.
****

The Chime Child was born
When the clock
struck three -
She was odder than plums
On an apple tree.

She listened to secrets
That swirled
in her head,
She spoke to the shadows
That circled her bed...

And the songs that she sang
Were so sad
And so sweet
The fairies came dancing
Around her feet.

****

(A Chime Child is born when the clock strikes
three, six, nine or twelve -
and some stories say they can see the Fairy-Folk.)

****

THE LISTENERS OF CLASS THIRTEEN.
****
(With thanks to Walter De La Mare's 'Listeners'.

"Is anybody there?" said the Teacher
Knocking on the classroom door...
And his words seemed to smell of ancient cough-sweets
In the dusty corridor;
And a bucket creaked on the narrow ledge
Above the Teacher's head -
And he wiggled the handle a second time:
"Is the door-monitor there?" he said.
But no one answered the Teacher,
No giggles disturbed the gloom,
Only that ominous creaking from
The horribly silent room.

Then he walloped the door even harder,
Swallowed a pill for his head -
"Tell them I came for Literacy Hour,
That I marked their work," he said.
Still not a sneeze reached the Teacher
As he leaned on the peeling wall -
So he gathered his books in his quivering arms,
Walked in. Let the bucket fall.
Now a wave of laughter crashed round his ears
While water sploshed like the Sea...
And the children cheered as the Teacher groaned:
"It's early Retirement for me!"

****

THE SINGERS OF ORCHARD CLOSE.
****

(Orchard Close - A Dead-End Where An Orchard Used To Grow.)

"An old-fashioned Wassail! Now that's the thing,
With costumes and tankards - and lanterns to swing;
Plus proper old carols
And tunes we can sing."

The whole crew agreed - so we jumped at the plan.
The songs were selected - we loaded the van
With fiddles and flutes
And a tall Scarecrow Man.

We clothed him in scarlet to make him look good -
But somebody grumbled - she tore off his hood.
She yelled: "He's the Spirit
Of Forest and Wood!"

So we made him a garland of pine-cones and leaves,
He wore a green jerkin with loose, knitted sleeves -
And berries like blood
For a giant who grieves.

The night of our Wassail, the crowds came to see -
So we sang from our hearts - Out of time and off key!
But the locals all smiled
Since the racket was free.

But just as we gathered round one, lonely tree...

A voice rose like birdsong. Such pure, liquid tones,
We froze for a moment. Grew silent as stones -
Then we followed that sound
Like a dog follows bones.

And when it was over, the people - they wept;
They filled up our cashbox with money they'd kept;
And later, they told us
That nobody slept...

But as I turned homewards, I saw, bright as day
An orchard of apple trees, misty and grey...
And a Green Man who waved
Bowed his head
Strode away.

****

THE POEM IN YOUR HAND.
****
(A Winter's Tale For Three Voices.)

Voice 1.   A stranger sat beside me in the
Cafe yesterday:
His eyes were ringed with shadows,
His face was gaunt and grey,
His voice was faint as echoes from
a forest far away.

Voice 2.   "Long years ago, a woman as unreal
as I must seem,
Appeared from mist and moonlight
Like a spirit - or a dream,
And her words fell fast as water, in a
cruel and bitter stream..."

Voice 1.   He told me of a poem that was
drenched with grief and dread,
His fingers clenched like talons...

Voice 2.   "And it haunts me still," he said.
"It rings me round with malice as it
howls inside my head."

Voice 1.   "You are frightened of a phantom. It's
a paper curse," I cried.
Just tear it up. Or burn it."
But the stranger only sighed...

Voice 2.   "I have no one else to help me. I have
nowhere else to hide."

Voice 2.   "Yet I did my best to warn you - but
you would not understand."

Voice 1.   Then he seized me. And he left me
(Give to Voice 1.)
                With the poem in my hand!
                It scorched me and it scarred me like
                a storm of desert sand.

Voice 1.   'So now I see those demons. Their
                laughter fills my ears.
                My nights are racked with torments,
                My days are soaked with tears."
                A woman leans towards me - and her
                laughter has no fears.

Voice 1.   "And yet I know you mock me, as a
                fool is bound to do.
                You think I'm sick. Or crazy.
                You think my tale's untrue..."
(Give the poem to Voice 3.)

Voice 3.   "So he left me with this poem -
                Which I now pass on to...YOU!"

(Give the Poem to the next victim and RUN!!)

****

'TIS THE SEASON TO BE SCARY.
****

"As darkness swoops down
As the day turns to night -
Can ANYONE give me a Seasonal Fright?"

Switch off the music and silence the phone;
Let candle-light flicker, let winter winds moan;

Let secrets be whispered of sinister things...
Vampires who rattle their leathery wings;

Monsters who lurk in the marsh and the river;
Phantoms who set all your senses a-quiver;

Creatures who creep from shadow-lands - there!
Just at the twist of the cobwebby stair;

Skeletons hidden for long, patient years;
Banshees who feast on your sorrows and fears;

Nightmares that haunt you and won't let you go;
Blood-thirsty Beasts who leave tracks in the snow;

Slobbering Horrors you half-wish to find;
Crawling from stories - to howl in your mind...

"Oh! Tease me with tales
Of the Crypt and the Axe-Man -
But NOTHING can scare me
As much as the
TAX-MAN!

****

THE HORRIBLE HAUNTING OF FIFI MOULD.

Poor Fifi Mould caught a feverish cold
Which set her a-sniffing and sneezing.
It jangled her head as she trudged off to bed
With whimpers, a wail and some wheezing.

At midnight, she woke. Was it steam? Was it smoke
In her mirror? Or had she been dreaming?
While the GHOST in the gloom took a spin round her room
In the hope of a squeal or some screaming.

But Fifi felt woozy, too bunged-up and snoozy
To manage a shake or a shiver.
So she tucked up all toasty, which troubled our ghostie -
(A spectre expects a quick quiver).

Then the flustery phantom flew back round the sanctum
To clatter the chains on his chest.
But each frantic rattle was losing the battle
And failing the House-Haunting Test.

When the Spectre-Inspector (with Terror-Detector)
Arrived to examine the Shrieks...
Old Fifi was snoring! Completely ignoring
The pitiful cackles and creaks.

So our Spook, sad to say, was sent far, far away
To appear in a scene from MacBeth -
While Fifi (who died) is a Spirit with Pride...
And a SNEEZE
That will scare you to death.

AAAAH-CHOOOO!

THE FRIDGE ON THE STAIR.
****

(I woke with this strange poem in my head - and I
had to finish it.
But it needed some sound effects - so please have fun!)

****

There's a fridge at the top of the steep castle stair -
Though last night, I'm certain
A fridge wasn't there.

It simply appeared without warning, today.
It's monstrous and old
And it's blocking my way.

And from its insides I am sure I can hear
The squeal of a rat,
Or a whimper of fear.

Or maybe the hoot of a mythical
owl,
Or else an unearthly
And ominous howl...

The brute starts to tilt, then it stumbles downstairs
On flat, rusty feet,
Two clattering pairs -

Now its door lurches open. It gapes like a cave!
Is that any way
For a fridge to behave?

It's lumbering closer. Its cold breath accosts me -
And an icy voice crackles:
"CAN SOMEONE DEFROST ME?"

****

CHRISTMAS PAST.
****

Open the album, summon the cast -
Let's live again
Our Christmas Past.

Here are the photos we yearly take...
My mother enjoying her slice of cake;
The cats asleep on my father's knee;
The laughing couples beside the tree;
The paper hats that don't quite fit;
The jumper your Mum took weeks to knit...

Your Dad, who loved the day so much;
Those tempting parcels we longed to touch;
Your Grans observing their Christmas truce;
The gadget that broke after one hour's use;
The girls with their favourite cuddly toys;
Our son with his drum kit - all that noise!

The baby's first taste of the whole affair,
With a halo of tinsel in his hair;
My bump, with only a month to go;
The time we truly saw some snow;
Your party tie, when you wore it new;
The awful year when we all had the flu';

And there's the star, where it's always hung...
And can you believe we looked so young!

So let the camera have its way,
Capture the spirit of today,
Then place the pictures on the shelves -
The smiling ghosts
Of our festive selves.

****

THE GHOST OF CHRISTMAS PAST.
****

I must have overdone it, with the pudding and the pies -
The stuffing and the turkey (which was twice the normal size).
Because, straight after dinner - I sat down and shut my eyes...

And found myself transported to a misty winter night.
I stumbled through the winding streets, I blundered left and right -
Until I reached a theatre that blazed with warmth and light...

I stepped inside. I watched a man I almost seemed to know
He mesmerised his audience with tales of long ago:
He spoke of haunted Christmases of orphans in the snow.

And there, with pen and passion, he was conjuring a Cast
Of Cratchits and of Phantoms from the darkness of the Past
To teach a mean old Miser how to change his life at last.

And now, the Reader turned into a broken-hearted Bride;
He took us to a homely boat - with Peggotty inside...
Or dragged us to the dreadful room where Nancy wept. And died.

His voice grew high and frightened as he told us of a child,
Who helped a hungry convict, in a graveyard bleak and wild;
But then we met Micawber who, despite bad fortune, smiled.

And next - the brave young Nickleby, who travelled far, to find
A teacher with a swishing cane, a cruel and vicious mind -
Then rescued Smike and left the school of misery behind.

So many lives, so many moods, so many vivid scenes -
The damp and twisted alleyway, where crafty Fagin leans;
The filthy Debtors' Prison where a faithful daughter cleans...

Then back again to Fezziwig who calls for festive fun;
And Bob, who's warmly welcomed when the dreary day is done -
While Tiny Tim still shouts out loud: "God Bless Us - Every One."

The book is closed.
I rise to cheer the Master of the Word;
I'll thank him for the stories
That have left my spirit stirred.
I'll gladly shake my Hero's hand - As time and space grow blurred...

****

I blink. I yawn. I'm in my room!
The tree-lights softly gleam...
While on my lap, the pages of: 'A Christmas Carol' seem
To tell me I have woken from
A DICKENS OF A DREAM.

****

ABOUT THE AUTHOR.
****

Clare Bevan used to be a teacher and she still loves visiting schools. Her first book won the Kathleen Fiddler Award, which was a wonderful thrill. Now she is best known for her children's poetry and her poems can be found in over one hundred anthologies.

More recently, she became Bracknell's First Poet Laureate, and her favourite poem was about the women who flew the Spitfire's in World War Two.

Clare lives in a cobwebby house (since she likes spiders) and her husband keeps her sane when she's scared of computers. Her hobbies are: performing her poems; wearing hats; feeding the birds in her garden, and riding a big, purple tricycle!

And of course - she loves Christmas.

****

Lightning Source UK Ltd.
Milton Keynes UK
UKHW020209131122
412093UK00007B/87